Nettie's Vegetarian Kitchen

Helene Giannakeas

NETTIE'S VEGETARIAN KITCHEN

BY

Nettie Cronish

SECOND STORY Press

CANADIAN CATALOGUING IN PUBLICATION

Cronish, Nettie, 1954-
Nettie's vegetarian kitchen

Includes index.
ISBN 0-929005-80-5

1. Vegetarian cookery. I. Title. II. Title: Vegetarian kitchen

TX837.C76 1996   641.5'636   C96-931605-4

Edited by Rhea Tregebov
Illustrations by Chum McLeod

Printed and bound in Canada

Published by
SECOND STORY PRESS
720 Bathurst Street Suite 301
Toronto Ontario
M5S 2R4

*This book is dedicated to the memory of
Emma Berkeley Urquhart Cronish,
November 6, 1994 – April 6, 1995,
our darling daughter who died of
sudden infant death syndrome.*

· ⅄ ·

Contents

ACKNOWLEDGMENTS

Thanks for inspiration, support and taste buds to: Kate Gammal, my distinguished recipe tester; to Pat Fletcher, Eve Weinberg, Gabriela Sousa Machado, Heather Scott, Helen Pasion, Gerry Pratt, Liz Greisman and Barbara Barron. Thanks also to the Hens' Teeth Food Buying Club: Marney Berube, Jane Larimer and Laurie Malabar; to The Big Carrot; The Women's Culinary Network Executive: Marilyn Crowley, Kate Gammal, Lili Sullivan and Heather Epp; to Second Story Press and Rhea Tregebov. And final thanks to my husband Jim and to Cameron, Mackenzie, Helen Cronish, Aunty Jenny, Edwin and Elaine Beallor, Cousin Suzie and Sari Neilson.

INTRODUCTION

The path to writing *Nettie's Vegetarian Kitchen* has been a long one. I suppose it started in 1981, when I began teaching cooking classes. I had been a vegetarian since 1974, and when I got a phone call from the Director of Toronto's Skills Exchange asking if I would teach a vegetarian cooking course, it seemed like a great idea. Here was an opportunity to think about exactly what I ate and to learn whether others would share my taste in cuisine.

At the end of the first course, a *Globe and Mail* reporter who had been in attendance approached me about writing an article on changing food trends. In preparation for the course I had begun to put my thoughts down on paper, so the newspaper article seemed like a natural next step. I was delighted by the offer, especially since the publicity for my catering company, Vegetarian Gourmet Delights, was welcome. The article was published and soon my phone was ringing off the hook. Before I knew it, I was cooking long into the night. The time came to expand, and I opened a deli in a health food store (Goldberries, on St. Nicholas Street in Toronto), where I cooked and catered for a year.

When the lease on the health food store was not renewed and the shelves were not restocked, I began for the first time to have leftovers. Jim (my life's partner) suggested I freeze them, and came up with the design for a Mister Natural funky vegetable label. Soon I was in the frozen vegetarian food business, distributing up to two thousand dinners a month to eighty stores.

When I had my first child, I could no longer maintain the catering cooking schedule I had previously sustained. I began teaching again, at Toronto's Big Carrot Health Food Store, developing courses that emphasized organically grown fruits and vegetables, soy foods, beans and grains. This experience confirmed how much I enjoyed teaching and meeting people whose diets were in transition. Teaching grounds me and keeps me from creating recipes with ninety-nine ingredients!

My understanding of vegetarian cooking expanded further when I got myself a job at the King Ranch health spa, which had just opened, as a demonstration vegetarian chef. I had never worked with so many other women in a kitchen and it was a supportive, non-competitive, hard-working, fun place to be. There I met and worked with Anne Lindsay who opened my eyes to the nutritional side of a recipe — her computer program to analyse nutritional values gave new meaning to my understanding of a recipe's "profile." Because King Ranch was committed to serving food that had 30% or less of its calories from fat, everything had to be measured and every recipe monitored for its fat content. I had thought vegetarian cooking to be quite low in fat, but in fact it isn't necessarily, especially when a lot of dairy products are used.

When the King Ranch went under, I became a founding member of the Women's Culinary Network, which was started by four women chefs and the Associate Food Editor of *Chatelaine* magazine. Although it has changed and evolved, today the Network has over 100 members, with chapters in other cities. (See page 19 for more information.)

So, fifteen years later I am still searching for delicious, easy to use ingredients that will excite my taste buds and nourish my soul. Diet is constantly evolving, and change is gradual. The aim of this book is to introduce people to vegetarian staples. I have tried to write concise, delicious, fast recipes that accommodate busy lives. Most of the people who attend my five week introductory cooking courses are not vegetarian. Over and over again, people remind me how pressured they are, how hard it is to consistently eat well. Change is tough. When people ask what I do and I respond with "I'm a vegetarian cooking teacher" they often will tell me how much they love to eat vegetables. I know then that I have twenty seconds to engage their interest in a non-threatening way, and to explain that there is more to vegetarian cooking than vegetables.

Vegetarian cooking is experiencing an upswing in popularity. Compared to a typical meat-and-potatoes meal, vegetarian food is usually higher in minerals, fibre and vitamins, lower in saturated fat, and easier to digest. A growing ecological awareness leads to a vegetarian awareness too. Land that grows beans, grains and vegetables will feed up to twenty-five times the number of people than the same piece of land used to raise beef. Looking at the worsening condition of the environment, it is not surprising that more and more people are considering vegetarian options.

Human hunger, religion, economics and good health are some of the reasons why people are changing their diet. I often refer to people who are lowering their consumption of animal foods as being "in transition" to a healthier diet. Food consumption categories can be quite confusing, so for the record, here are three basic categories:

Lacto-ovo vegetarians avoid all animal flesh but they do use eggs (ovo) and dairy products (lacto). Lacto vegetarians exclude animal flesh and eggs and use dairy products. Ovo vegetarians use eggs but avoid dairy products.

Vegans avoid all foods of animal origin including dairy foods, eggs, honey and gelatin. (Gelatin is made from the bones and connective tissues of animals.)

The *macrobiotic* diet is based on the Japanese concepts of yin and yang. It is dairy-free, but it may include fish. This diet puts an emphasis on following seasonal foods and on eating foods locally grown. Foods are classified according to their expansive and contractive qualities, for example, alcohol and sugar are "yin," expansive; meats and salt are "yang," contractive. The goal of the macrobiotic diet is to find a balance of foods closer to the centre.

I find macrobiotic cooking too time consuming — and I enjoy grated cheese in many a casserole. My diet, and this cookbook, uses small amounts of dairy. But tailor these recipes to your own preferences. Soy milk can be interchanged for regular milk, good-tasting nutritional yeast for grated cheese, and puréed tofu for eggs. Desserts can easily be converted into lower fat versions when fruit purées such as apple butter are used to replace most of the oil or butter listed as ingredients. Flax seeds can be used to replace eggs in baking (see page 203 for details).

The biggest worry people have regarding a vegetarian diet is the amount of protein — are they eating enough of the right foods? This insecurity originates from the fact that animal foods contain all eight essential amino acids not manufactured by our body, while plant foods lack some of those essential amino acids. Earlier theories taught that it was necessary to complement our proteins, to combine beans with grains or dairy products to give us all eight essential amino acids. This approach is well-reflected in established ethnic cuisines. New nutritional information suggests that a varied, well-rounded diet provides all the essential amino acids without any need to eat beans and grains in combination all the time. Many people new to vegetarian cooking may choose to start out carefully "complementing proteins." However, once you become accustomed to the many delicious and exciting ingredients of a vegetarian kitchen, your common sense and exploratory taste buds will let you take off.

So, if you are looking for easy to follow, luscious recipes that take under forty-five minutes to prepare, this is the book for you.

About the Nutritional Analyses

Nettie's recipes have been computer-analysed using the program *Food Processor II* to show the number of calories and the amount in grams of protein, carbohydrates and fat for each recipe. Those who are eliminating animals products from their diet are particularly conscious of the amount of vitamin B12, calcium, iron and zinc in their daily nutrient intake. Therefore when a recipe contains a significant amount of one of these targeted nutrients, the nutrient value has been highlighted. For example, Nettie's *Tahini Miso Dip* (page 42) is a particularly good source of zinc, so the zinc value (1 mg) is noted just after the nutrient analysis.

What a great pleasure it is for me to see Nettie incorporate a large array of soy foods such as tofu, tempeh and miso in her recipes. Soy foods are fast becoming recognized as playing a significant role in the prevention and treatment of a number of chronic illnesses. Studies have suggested that the chemical compound isoflavone, which occurs naturally in soybean protein, directly lowers the "bad" cholesterol LDL. In addition, menopausal women may find soy products helpful in easing menopausal symptoms. Studies have shown that rural Japanese women, whose diets traditionally contain a large percentage of soy foods, have very little menopausal discomfort. They also have low rates of osteoporosis, coronary heart disease and breast cancer.

Nettie's use of sea vegetables, which provide a remarkable source of valuable nutrients, is also a nutritional plus. Sea vegetables contain an abundant supply of essential vitamins. They also contain trace minerals which may be sadly lacking in our diet, since modern agricultural methods and the loss of topsoil deplete such minerals in our conventional fruits and vegetables.

You might find that some of Nettie's recipes appear to have a greater fat content than expected. However, a closer examination of how fat fits in our diet reveals a different story. Here is an example of how *Tofu Cream Cheese Spread* (page 36) fits into your daily menu planning. A one tablespoon serving of Nettie's *Tofu Cream Cheese Spread*, using light cream cheese, contains 30 calories and 3 grams of fat, providing 90% of its calories from fat. If you are maintaining your weight at 2,000 calories per day, and are following the recommended intake of 25% of calories from fat, that means you should consume 500 calories per day from fat. Since there are 9 calories per gram of fat, your total recommended fat intake is *56 grams of fat per day*. Three grams of fat from the *Tofu Cream Cheese Spread* fits well into your meal plan.

And what if you use the *Tofu Cream Cheese Spread* on some bread or crackers? Using 1½ tablespoons of the spread on a multigrain bagel with sliced tomato, your sandwich contains 215 calories with 6 grams of fat. And 25% of your calories for this sandwich come from fat. It is important to focus not only on the total grams of fat in a given food, but also on *what else we are eating with that meal*. The sliced tomato and bagel with the spread will bring the percentage of calories from fat down from 80% to 25%. This is why I'd rather see my clients count the grams of fat they consume per day than have them looking only at the percentage of fat in a particular food.

As a vegetarian nutritionist, I try to provide my clients with recipes that are not only healthful but easy to follow — and tasty. *Nettie's Vegetarian Kitchen* offers you delicious whole food cuisine that is fast, nourishing and full of flavour.

Enjoy!

— *Bonnie Kumer, RD*

The Women's Culinary Network

The Women's Culinary Network affirms the collective and individual empowerment of women. It is our intention to create a medium for communication that allows us to network, socialize, support and educate each other, building upon our accumulated knowledge and skills.

Our organization was founded in 1990 by four women chefs who were working at the King Ranch Spa and by the Associate Food Editor of *Chatelaine* magazine. We wanted to meet and work with other women in the food industry in a mutually supportive and goal-oriented environment. Our common purpose was to share professional experience, knowledge and information that could expand our horizons, and to have a good time in the process.

Five years later, we want to lend our support to individuals, regardless of whether you are just graduating from a course, running a successful business or working in some part of the food industry. We aim to fill a niche that will allow us to pool our resources and to celebrate each others' efforts, ambitions and successes.

Our membership is growing. We currently have 100 members ranging from chefs, food consultants, nutritionists, cooking teachers and food writers to business owners, students, home economists and product developers. We meet bi-monthly from September to May, usually in a social setting, to encourage discussion, update information and to provide an excellent opportunity to enjoy professional camaraderie.

The Women's Culinary Network
11 Dunloe Road
Toronto ON M4V 2W4
Phone: (416) 483 7114   Fax: (416) 487 3849

Vegetarian Cooking Classes

I offer demonstration and hands-on cooking classes as a part of making people better consumers. Classes focus on cooking with new ingredients, proper storage and fridge life. Clients have ranged from corporations with a wellness department to half-a-dozen friends gathered together.

Topics include:
- how to cook beans and grains
- an introduction to soy foods (tofu, tempeh and miso)
- how to prepare delicious vegetable stock
- elegant holiday meals
- what do kids eat? (toddlers to teens)
- setting up a natural foods kitchen

Setting Up Your Natural Foods Kitchen

When I used to go over to people's houses to assist them in setting up natural foods kitchens, I was constantly amazed at how long people would store certain ingredients: the dull, dried-out surfaces of these foodstuffs simply begged to be thrown out. People seem to become emotionally attached to certain foods and brands, and feel the need to maintain a constant supply in their home. No one had much of an explanation as to why they needed to keep a minimum of 6 cup-a-soups (chicken noodle) on their shelves.... Although I was concerned about how long past the expiry date these cherished items had been there, I understood how hard it was to change the habits of a lifetime.

Once we'd discarded the outdated materials, leaving cupboards bare (and washed), we would plan menus for a month and assemble a list of basics. As I tried to listen to people's needs — and they tried to listen to my suggestions — I realized just how tough it was for some people to give up their ingredients, so my advice is: *don't*. Wait till you're ready for that moment when you decide to buy organic dried apricots at considerably more expense than the commercial brand. So when you are feeling ready for a change, or adventurous, here are a few suggestions. Remember that these are just guidelines.

ESSENTIAL EQUIPMENT

WASHING AND CUTTING VEGETABLES
1 stainless steel or carbon steel vegetable knife 9"/ 23 cm
1 paring knife
sharpening stone
1 large cutting board
1 small cutting board
strainer — rinse vegetables and grains
brush to scrub vegetables and grains
lettuce spinner

POTS AND PANS (STAINLESS STEEL OR CAST IRON)
2 L saucepan with lid — sauces, reheat leftovers
4 L saucepan with lid — soups, boil grains and noodles
6 L saucepan with lid — stews, beans, vegetables
1 stainless steel pressure cooker
1 small skillet
1 large skillet
wok with stand — carbon steel, stir-fry, steam
2 flame tamers
suribachi — mortar and pestle set (grinds nuts and seeds)
large pot

UTENSILS	USEFUL EQUIPMENT	ELECTRIC
whisk	bamboo vegetable steamer	food processor
spatula	stainless steel steamer	toaster oven
chopsticks	teapot and strainer	blender
vegetable peeler	kitchen scale	
juicer	timer	
wooden spoons	4 mixing bowls of different sizes	

BAKING NEEDS
measuring cups	muffin tray
measuring spoons	2 bowls
cookie sheet	cake pan
pastry brush	quiche dish

STAPLES TO KEEP ON HAND

These are the basics. With them on hand I can always put together something fairly interesting to eat: all I need to add are the fresh vegetables and tofu. The herbs and spice list, which is lengthy, allows me to prepare basic dishes from a fairly wide range of cuisines including Mexican, Italian, French, Indian and Chinese.

OILS
canola
extra virgin olive oil
toasted sesame oil

DRY GOODS
baking powder
baking soda
basmati rice
black beans
bread crumbs
brown rice
bulgur
cornmeal
fusilli pasta
good-tasting nutritional yeast
kasha (buckwheat groats)
lentils
millet
quinoa
soba noodles
sushi rice
unbleached white flour
whole wheat flour
wild rice

VINEGARS
balsamic vinegar
red wine vinegar
rice vinegar
white wine vinegar

DAIRY AND SOY
2% milk
butter
eggs
goat cheese
low-fat yogurt
miso
Monterey Jack cheese
Parmesan cheese (freshly grated)
seitan
soy milk
tofu

CANNED GOODS
artichoke hearts
black olives
capers
coconut milk
garbanzo beans (chick-peas)
green olives
kidney beans
pinto beans
salsa
tomato juice
tomato paste
tomato sauce
whole peeled potatoes

NUTS AND SEEDS
(store in refrigerator)
almond nut butter
almonds
cashews
peanut butter
pecans
pumpkin seeds
sesame seeds
sunflower seeds
tahini
walnuts

SEA VEGETABLES
nori sheets
arame
kombu
hijiki
agar-agar flakes

DRIED HERBS AND SPICES
basil
cardamom
cayenne
chili powder
cinnamon
cumin seeds
curry powder
dill
ground coriander
ground cumin
marjoram
nutmeg
oregano
paprika
sea salt
thyme
turmeric
whole black peppercorns

FRESH PRODUCE
carrots
celery
fresh basil
fresh parsley
garlic
gingerroot
green onions
lemons
lettuce
small potatoes
spinach
sprouts
sweet potatoes
tomatoes
Vidalia onions
zucchini

CONDIMENTS

Barbados molasses
curry paste
Dijon mustard
ketchup
mirin
pickled ginger
pickles
soy mayonnaise
soy sauce
umebushi plum paste
wasabi

DRIED FRUITS

apricots
dates
prunes
raisins

MISCELLANEOUS

dried mushrooms
edible flowers (lavender,
nasturtium, marigold, pansy)
fruit leather
parchment paper
pita bread
sun-dried tomatoes
tortilla chips
vanilla extract
vegetable bouillon cubes

FREEZER GOODS

cooked beans
filo dough
flax seeds
pizza dough
tempeh
tortillas

SWEETENERS

apple sauce
honey
maple syrup
prune purée
sucanat

SUGGESTED MENUS

GOURMET DINNER

Mushroom Pâté
Picnic Nori Rolls
Miso Soup with Sea Vegetables
Goat Cheese Spinach Casserole (with a cooked grain)
Tempeh Sloppy Joes (with a cooked noodle)
Carrot Cake

SOY TONIGHT!

Baked Garlic
Quinoa Salad with Roasted Nuts
Tofu Stroganoff
All Purpose Pasta
Coconut Cake

FESTIVE SOLSTICE MEAL

Roasted Eggplant Dip
Garlic Soup with Potatoes & Cumin
Marinated Tofu Salad
Vegetarian Moussaka
Wild Rice with Pine Nuts
Gingersnaps

WINTER DINNER

Tofu Cream Cheese Spread with Garlic & Herbs
Pot-Luck Chili
Tabbouleh Kasha
Thai Broccoli
Date Bread

EARLY SPRING DINNER

Tangy Hummus
Buckwheat Potato Pancakes
Ratatouille
Lemon Poppy Seed Cake

SUMMER BRUNCH

Salsa Tempeh Dip
Broccoli with Roasted Peppers, Olives & Feta Cheese
Basmati Herb Pilaf
Peanut Butter Cookies

LATE SUMMER DINNER

Spinach Chestnut Dip
Hot & Sour Buckwheat Noodle Salad
Bean Pie with Millet Crust
Apple Crisp

FALL DINNER

Sweet Pea Sesame Spread
Apricot Lentil Soup
Lime Quinoa Salad
Curried Tofu in Pita Bread
Apple Crisp

APPETIZERS

APPETIZERS

WHEN YOU ARE INVITING guests to your home for a meal, appetizers are a must. When people start to relax, they realize how hungry they are. Many people don't eat three meals a day, and in our culture the big meal of the day is usually supper. Also, if you are serving alcoholic beverages, it's a good idea to have some food on hand.... Foods that are flexible and that blend easily with your main course should guide your choice.

When we do eat an appetizer, we want to add nutritionally balanced ingredients to the meal, rather than just adding extra calories.

An appetizer like *Baked Garlic* can be used as a spread instead of butter or oil. Many of the dips I have included in this section can be spooned into mini pitas or scooped into hollowed-out veggie slices. The *Mushroom Pâté, Salsa Tempeh Dip* and *Sweet Pea Sesame Spread* all deserve a big platter of corn chips and sliced carrots, zucchini and celery. They are also terrific open-faced sandwich spreads, and are fast and easy to prepare.

· ✕ ·

GARLIC CUISINE

I never travel without garlic. Aside from its culinary uses, garlic has many medicinal qualities: it cleanses the intestinal flora of harmful organisms and possesses antiseptic and antibiotic properties. Garlic was used during both World Wars to control gangrene and infection; it was also used by gardeners as a natural pesticide. Garlic has been referred to as "nature's miracle medicine chest."

Garlic (*Allium Sativum*) has been with us for thousands of years. The plant is a member of the lily family and is thought to be from the desert region of Siberia. It travelled to Egypt via Asia Minor through the migrations of nomadic tribes, and to Eastern Asia from India, thence to Europe via the trade routes. Garlic grew wild in North and South America as well. The aboriginal peoples ate it as a vegetable and were familiar with its medicinal properties.

There are two varieties of garlic: white- and pink-skinned. The white-skinned bulbs have a stronger flavour and are not as sweet as the pink-skinned variety. I look for bulbs with large cloves, usually about twelve on a head. Always press the outer clove to ensure they are firm and solid, not old and dry. One large clove yields 1 to 1½ teaspoons of chopped garlic. Garlic is best stored in a cool, dry ventilated place.

There are many ways to prepare garlic — mincing, slicing, coarsely chopping, pressing and puréeing. How you use it depends on your taste and the recipe you're using. Sometimes pressing garlic yields a taste stronger than what you may want. Garlic's strong taste is from sulphur compounds that are released when the cell membranes are broken which oxidize upon contact with air. The more forcefully the membranes are broken down, the stronger the smell and taste. Therefore, garlic put through a press or crushed and mashed will be stronger tasting than garlic that is chopped or sliced, and much stronger than garlic that is simmered whole.

The best antidote to garlic breath is raw parsley. Chew two sprigs; the high amount of chlorophyll found in other greens also works well as a deodorizer.

BAKED GARLIC

Move over butter and margarine! This is a healthy substitute, whether you spread it on bread or on potatoes. Mash with a fork, eat whole baked cloves, add to sandwiches and casseroles — this is a terrific way to eat lots of garlic and enjoy its sweet, unmistakable flavour. It will brighten up anybody's dressings or marinades. This is as subtle as it gets! As you squeeze your cloves of baked garlic onto your crackers or croutons, you will be pleasantly surprised by how mild this recipe tastes, the stronger flavours being tempered by cooking.

PREPARATION TIME: 5 MINUTES
COOKING TIME: 1 HOUR

4 heads fresh garlic
¼ *cup* olive oil *50 mL*
4 sprigs fresh thyme
sea salt to taste
freshly ground pepper to taste

Preheat oven to 325°F (160°C).

Cut 4 squares of aluminum foil large enough to thoroughly enclose one head of garlic. Using a serrated knife, cut off tops of heads of garlic. Place a head of garlic on each square and drizzle on oil. Add thyme, salt and pepper.

Seal garlic in foil. The edges should be sealed, but there should be sufficient space around the garlic so that it can expand and simmer in its own juices.

Bake for 1 hour.

Remove from foil enclosure. Place heads on lettuce-lined platter. Separate the cloves, squeezing the garlic onto rice cakes, crackers, or vegetables.

MAKES 4 SERVINGS.

Keeps 4 days covered in the refrigerator.

Per Serving:
calories 124
protein - g
carbohydrates 1 g
fat 14 g

Tofu Cream Cheese Spread
with Garlic & Herbs

*I have served this on crackers, open-faced sandwiches, stuffed
in a pita with sprouts, squeezed into the hollow of a celery stalk,
sliced or just used as a dip. No one guesses at the presence of tofu —
you can experiment with the amounts of cream cheese and tofu,
using more tofu, say 12 oz (375 g) to 4 oz (125 g) cream cheese.
Some people notice; some don't. My mother, Helen Cronish, serves this
dip to her poker club when it's her turn to serve. They have been playing cards for forty years and are watching their cholesterol.*

PREPARATION TIME: 10 MINUTES

8 oz tofu *250 g*
8 oz cream cheese *250 g*
2 cloves garlic, minced
3 Tbsp chopped fresh coriander *45 mL*
½ tsp dried thyme *2 mL*
½ tsp dried basil *2 mL*
1 Tbsp lemon juice *15 mL*
1 Tbsp chopped chives *15 mL*
½ tsp freshly ground pepper *2 mL*
¼ tsp salt *1 mL*

Using food processor, purée tofu until smooth. Add
cream cheese, garlic, coriander, thyme, basil, lemon juice,
chives, pepper and salt.

Cover and put in refrigerator.

MAKES 2 CUPS (500 mL).

Keeps 3 days covered in the refrigerator.

Per 1 Tablespoon Serving:
calories 31
protein 1 g
carbohydrates 1 g
fat 3 g

Sweet Pea Sesame Spread

A luscious spread that can fill a celery cavity or stick to a cracker and glisten with goodness. Delicious as an open-faced sandwich spread, suitable for tortilla chip dipping. The bright green sparkles with good taste.

PREPARATION TIME: 20 MINUTES

¼ cup sesame seeds *50 mL*
3 Tbsp vegetable stock or water *45 mL*
1 large onion, chopped
2 cloves garlic, minced
1 (10 oz) package frozen (small) peas *280 g*
¼ cup mirin or dry sherry *50 mL*
1 tsp salt *5 mL*
1 Tbsp good-tasting nutritional yeast *15 mL*
1 tsp lemon juice *5 mL*

Toast sesame seeds in medium, dry, non-stick saucepan over medium-high heat, stirring until golden, 5 minutes. Set aside.

Heat vegetable stock or water in same pot over medium heat. Cook onion and garlic until softened, 5 minutes.

Add peas, mirin and salt. Cover, reduce heat to low and cook until peas are soft, 5 minutes.

Stir in yeast and lemon juice.

Purée peas in food processor or blender. Add sesame seeds and process until well blended.

Serve chilled.

MAKES 2 CUPS (500 mL).

Keeps 3 days covered in the refrigerator.

Per ¼ Cup Serving:
calories 78
protein 3 g
carbohydrates 9 g
fat 2 g

Nutrient Highlights:
calcium 64 mg

Fig Butter

This dip tastes incredibly rich. Figs are high in calcium and iron, and this spread, served with fresh fruit and crackers, is a delicious way to replace conventional fat-laden spreads.

PREPARATION TIME: 5 MINUTES
COOKING TIME: 45 MINUTES

1 ½ cups dried figs, chopped *375 mL*
1 cup apple juice *250 mL*
1 cinnamon stick
3 Tbsp lemon juice *45 mL*
1 Tbsp grated lemon rind *15 mL*

Combine figs, apple juice, cinnamon stick, lemon rind and juice in saucepan. Bring to a boil, cover.

Reduce heat and simmer, stirring occasionally for about 45 minutes, or until figs are very soft.

Remove cinnamon stick and purée in food processor or blender until smooth.

MAKES 1 CUP (250 mL).
Keeps up to 2 weeks covered in the refrigerator.

Per 1 Tbsp Serving:
calories 44
protein .5 g
carbohydrates 11 g
fat - g

SALSA TEMPEH DIP

*I didn't know what to do with some thawed leftover tempeh, so I
steamed it. Because it has very little taste on its own, I dipped a finger
of it in some salsa (beside the corn chips), added a few more ingredients,
and created a dip. Use fresh chili powder — it makes all the difference!
(See page 140 for an introduction to tempeh.)*

PREPARATION TIME: 20 MINUTES

8 oz tempeh, cubed *250 g*
3 Tbsp canola oil *45 mL*
¼ cup water *50 mL*
2 cloves garlic, crushed
1 tsp chili powder *5 mL*
2 tsp ground cumin *10 mL*
2 tsp soy sauce *10 mL*
1 cup medium salsa *250 mL*

Steam tempeh over boiling water for 15 minutes.
Purée tempeh, oil, water, garlic, chili, cumin and soy
sauce in food processor or blender until slightly chunky.
Pour into bowl and stir in salsa. Chill well before serving.

MAKES 2 CUPS (500 ML).

Keeps 3 days in the refrigerator.
TIP: To personalize this, use homemade salsa with a heat level you enjoy.

Per ¼ Cup Serving:
calories 130
protein 7 g
carbohydrates 5 g
fat 9 g

Nutrient Highlights:
iron 2 mg

Tahini Miso Dip

*A great dip for chips, pitas and crunchy raw vegetables, its taste
is distinct and smooth. To use as a salad dressing,
thin with up to ¼ cup (50 mL) hot water.*

PREPARATION TIME: 20 MINUTES

1 ½ cups tahini *375 mL*
2 tsp finely chopped garlic *10 mL*
1 Tbsp finely chopped basil *15 mL*
2 Tbsp chopped parsley *25 mL*
2 Tbsp barley miso *25 mL*
2 scallions, chopped
¾ cup water *175 mL*

Roast tahini in heavy skillet over a medium-high heat, stirring constantly, for 5 minutes. Tahini will turn a golden brown when it is done. Set aside in mixing bowl to cool.

When tahini is warm, add garlic, basil, parsley, miso and scallions. Mix well. Cool.

Add water in small amounts, slowly blending it until the mixture is smooth and creamy. If the tahini is very thick, use another ¼ cup (50 mL) of water.

MAKES 2 CUPS (500 mL).

Keeps 2 days covered in the refrigerator.

Per 1 Tablespoon Serving:
calories 71
protein 2 g
carbohydrates 2 g
fat 6 g

Nutrient Highlights:
zinc 1 mg

Ginger Almond Dip

The combination of fresh gingerroot, garlic and almond nut butter creates a taste sensation on the palate. Add to a stir fry or use in place of mustard in a sandwich — or even by itself. Use a tablespoon or so to add flavour to salad dressings and sauces.

PREPARATION TIME: 10 MINUTES

1 cup smooth almond nut butter *250 mL*
2 Tbsp hot water *25 mL*
1 Tbsp grated fresh gingerroot *15 mL*
1 clove garlic
1 small onion, grated
2 Tbsp lemon juice *25 mL*
2 Tbsp soy sauce *25 mL*
1 tsp honey *5 mL*

Mix together almond butter and water in food processor or blender. Add gingerroot, garlic, onion, lemon juice, soy sauce and honey; process until smooth.

Add more water as necessary to reach desired consistency.

MAKES 1 CUP (250 ML).

Keeps 4 days covered in the refrigerator.

Per 1 Tbsp Serving:
calories 104
protein 3 g
carbohydrates 5 g
fat 9 g

Nutrient Highlights:
calcium 44 mg

SPINACH CHESTNUT DIP

I yearn for chestnuts all fall; they strike me as seasonal food. But canned water chestnuts are always available. The combination of spinach, sour cream, yogurt, watercress and dill makes for a refreshing, bright green, you-know-it's-healthy dish. I especially like dipping freshly baked dark rye bread into this dip and mopping it up.

PREPARATION TIME: 20 MINUTES

1 Tbsp butter *15 mL*
1 bunch fresh spinach, chopped *1 L*
1 cup sour cream *250 mL*
½ cup yogurt *125 mL*
½ cup watercress, chopped *125 mL*
1 clove garlic, minced
½ cup water chestnuts, chopped *125 mL*
1 Tbsp chopped fresh dill *15 mL*
½ tsp salt *2 mL*

Melt butter in cast-iron frying pan on medium heat. Add spinach and cook until just wilted, about 2 minutes.

Press any excess water out of spinach; place in mixing bowl.

Add sour cream, yogurt, watercress, garlic, water chestnuts, dill and salt.

Mix well, or purée in food processor for 2 minutes.

MAKES 2 CUPS (500 mL).

Keeps 3 days in the refrigerator.
*TIP: Thin with vegetable stock to desired consistency
to make a cold soup.*

Per ¼ Cup Serving:
calories 100
protein 3 g
carbohydrates 6 g
fat 8 g

Nutrient Highlights:
calcium 108 mg

Cayenne Bean Dip

Stuff celery with this dip. Spread on pieces of bread, open-faced sandwiches, crackers, your finger.... Use whatever fresh herb is available either from the market or your garden.

PREPARATION TIME: 15 MINUTES

1 cup cooked beans (navy, red
or white kidney beans) *250 mL*
1 small onion, finely chopped
1 clove garlic, minced
2 Tbsp lemon juice *25 mL*
1 tsp olive oil *5 mL*
½ tsp cayenne *2 mL*
⅓ cup water *75 mL*
2 Tbsp chopped fresh basil *25 mL*
¼ tsp salt *1 mL*
¼ tsp pepper *1 mL*

Combine beans, onion, garlic, lemon juice, olive oil, cayenne and enough water to make a smooth, spreadable paste in food processor or blender.
Season with basil, salt and pepper.

MAKES 2 ½ CUPS (625 mL).

Keeps 3 days in the refrigerator.

Per Serving:
calories 42
protein 2 g
carbohydrates 7 g
fat 1 g

TANGY HUMMUS

This has got to be one of my very favourite foods. It is Mid-eastern in origin and has a chick-pea/sesame taste, flavoured with garlic and lemon juice. You can prepare it a day in advance, and serve as a sandwich spread or dip for fresh vegetables.
(See page 105 for instructions on cooking chick-peas.)

PREPARATION TIME: 10 MINUTES

2 cups cooked chick-peas *500 mL*
¼ cup bean liquid *50 mL*
¼ cup lemon juice *50 mL*
2 cloves garlic, minced
½ tsp sea salt *2 mL*
3 Tbsp tahini *45 mL*
2 Tbsp olive oil *25 mL*
1 Tbsp chopped parsley *15 mL*

Purée chick-peas and bean liquid in food processor or blender. Add lemon juice, garlic, salt and tahini. Purée to form a thick paste.

Transfer to serving dish. Stir in olive oil partially, sprinkle with parsley before serving.

MAKES 1½ CUPS (375 mL).

Keeps 2 days.

Per ¼ Cup Serving:
calories 179
protein 6 g
carbohydrates 18 g
fat 10 g

Nutrient Highlights:
calcium 42 mg
iron 2 mg
zinc 2 mg

ROASTED EGGPLANT DIP

*Eggplant reminds me of caviar. This dip slides luxuriously down
the throat, leaving one sighing with pleasure. I often buy mini pitas,
slice their tops off and fill the cavity with this dip and
add a sprig of cilantro (alias coriander).*

PREPARATION TIME: 15 MINUTES
COOKING TIME: 30 MINUTES

½ lb whole eggplant 250 g
1 tsp ground cumin seed 5 mL
pinch salt
pinch cayenne
1 Tbsp lemon juice 15 mL
½ tsp chopped fresh thyme 2 mL
(or ¼ tsp/1 mL dried thyme)
1 tomato, finely chopped
¼ cup coarsely chopped fresh cilantro 50 mL
½ cup low-fat yogurt 125 mL

Preheat oven to 350°F (180°C).

Place whole eggplant in a shallow baking dish. Prick and
roast for 30 minutes, until tender when pierced with the
point of a knife. Remove and allow to cool for 10 minutes.

Remove and discard skin and stem of eggplant.

Purée eggplant pulp in blender or food processor.
Combine with cumin, salt, cayenne, lemon juice and thyme.

Stir in tomato and coriander.

Allow mixture to cool completely, then fold in yogurt.

MAKES 2 CUPS (500 ML).

Keeps 3 days in the refrigerator.
TIP: Grill eggplant for a rich smoky flavour and proceed with recipe as above.

Per ¼ Cup Serving:
calories 20
protein 1 g
carbohydrates 4 g
fat - g

MUSHROOM PÂTÉ

It does resemble chopped liver! You can use different types of mushrooms — oyster, fresh shiitake, button or portobello. The creamy texture lends itself to so many things: spread, sandwich filling, pita stuffer with sprouts. This simple recipe can be prepared a day in advance. Decorate with sprigs of parsley and cherry tomatoes.

PREPARATION TIME: 15 MINUTES

3 Tbsp canola oil *45 mL*
2 onions, chopped
½ lb mushrooms, thinly sliced *250 g*
½ tsp dried thyme *2 mL*
½ cup sunflower seeds or almonds, finely ground *125 mL*
½ tsp sea salt *2 mL*
1 Tbsp good-tasting nutritional yeast *15 mL*

Heat oil in large skillet over medium-high heat. Cook onion 3 minutes until brown.

Add mushrooms and cook for 7 minutes longer, stirring often, until mushrooms are browned and water is evaporated. Add thyme.

Put mixture into blender or food processor and purée. Add sunflower seeds, salt and yeast. Purée until coarse.

Put into plastic-wrap lined serving dish (approximately 3" x 6"/7.5 x 15 cm), cover.

Chill at least 30 minutes or up to 2 days.

MAKES 1½ CUPS (375 mL) OR 3" X 6" (7.5 X 15 CM) PÂTÉ.

Keeps 3 days in the refrigerator.

Per Serving:
calories 90
protein 2 g
carbohydrates 6 g
fat 7 g

HOT & SPICY GUACAMOLE

*I don't enjoy hot food any more, but if you do, use 2 jalapeño peppers.
I've also used this dip as a salad dressing, and I like to pour it over
grain/sprout stuffed pitas. I'm a sucker for the bright green colour.*

PREPARATION TIME: 20 MINUTES

4 ripe avocados
¼ *cup* lemon juice *50 mL*
¼ *cup* finely chopped onion *50 mL*
¼ *cup* chopped fresh coriander *50 mL*
2 tomatoes, coarsely chopped
1 jalapeño, seeded, finely chopped
1 tsp salt *5 mL*

Cut avocados in half lengthwise, remove pits, and scoop
out the pulp. In medium-sized bowl, mash avocado with a
silver fork or wooden spoon.
Add lemon juice, onions and coriander.
Add tomatoes to avocado along with jalapeño and salt.
Stir everything together. Chill.

MAKES 4 CUPS (1 L).

Keeps 1 day in the refrigerator.

Per ¼ Cup Serving:
calories 78
protein 1 g
carbohydrates 4 g
fat 7 g

SOUPS

Soups

Vegetable Stock is the cornerstone of the kitchen. Spend as much time as you can and prepare litres of the stuff. It will freeze well: freeze small amounts in an ice cube tray (fill ¾ full only, it will expand), and larger amounts in various sized containers. While I encourage my students to use whatever vegetables they have in their kitchen, I have found that cabbage, cauliflower and broccoli have strong flavours that do not blend well into a vegetable stock. These vegetables can also give stock an unpleasant odour, so I'd advise that you avoid them.

Most of us find that soups taste better the second day. Time allows the flavours to mellow and mesh, and reheating your soup concentrates the flavours even more.

Apricot Lentil Soup is delicious hot or cold. If you can afford to purchase organic apricots, you'll find that their flavour will burst in your mouth. Many of these soup recipes can easily turn from soups into stews. Simply add extra cooked grains or beans, and you have a thicker soup. Whether you prepare *Beet and Cabbage Borscht, Garlic Soup with Potatoes & Cumin,* or *Miso,* you will be serving bowls of tangy, tasty goodness that can be made into meals themselves.

VEGETABLE STOCK

What would any kitchen be without fresh and frozen vegetable stock?
I can't count the number of times I have been reading a "vegetarian"
recipe only to come across a measurement for chicken stock!
This stock is easy to prepare and delicious just by itself.

PREPARATION TIME: 30 MINUTES
COOKING TIME: 30 MINUTES

2 Tbsp olive oil *25 mL*
2 cloves garlic, minced
2 onions, sliced
2 leeks (white only) trimmed, sliced and washed
4 carrots, chopped
1 potato, chopped
4 celery stalks, sliced
6 tomatoes, quartered
½ lb mushrooms, wiped and sliced *250 g*
⅔ cup dried lentils *150 mL*
6 sprigs parsley
4 sprigs basil
4 bay leaves
2 tsp salt *10 mL*
½ tsp black peppercorns *2 mL*
10 cups water *2.5 L*

Heat oil in a 3 quart (3L saucepan) saucepan over medium heat. Add garlic, onions and leeks. Cook 5 minutes, or until softened.

Stir in carrots, potato and celery; cook for another 10 minutes.

Stir in tomatoes, mushrooms, lentils, parsley, basil, bay leaves, salt and pepper. Cover with water. Bring to a boil and skim.

Reduce heat to medium-low and simmer, covered, for 30 minutes, skimming occasionally.

Strain through fine sieve and cool before storing in container in refrigerator.

MAKES 10 CUPS (2.5 L).

Keeps up to 5 days in the refrigerator.
TIP: Freeze stock in ice cube trays. Once frozen, store cubes in freezer bags. Each cube yields approximately 2 Tbsp (25 mL) stock.

Per 1 Cup Serving:
calories 141
protein 6 g
carbohydrates 24 g
fat 3 g

Nutrient Highlights:
calcium 47 mg
iron 3 mg
zinc 1 mg

Apricot Lentil Soup

I prefer to use organic dried apricots: they resemble shrivelled up buttons and cost an arm and a leg. But the flavour! It bursts in your mouth like a morning song. Delicious hot or cold.

PREPARATION TIME: 15 MINUTES
COOKING TIME: 45 MINUTES

1 ½ cups   dried green lentils   *375 mL*
10 cups   vegetable stock or water   *2.5 L*
1 cup   chopped dried apricots   *250 mL*
2 Tbsp   safflower oil   *25 mL*
1   large onion, chopped
1   green pepper, chopped
1   red pepper, chopped
2 cups   chopped tomatoes (fresh or canned)   *500 mL*
½ tsp   cinnamon   *2 mL*
¼ tsp   ground cardamom   *1 mL*
¼ tsp   cayenne   *1 mL*
1 Tbsp   paprika   *15 mL*
2 tsp   salt   *10 mL*
2 Tbsp   chopped fresh parsley   *25 mL*

Rinse lentils, and then bring to a boil in water or stock. Reduce heat and simmer, covered, for 20 minutes.

Add apricots and simmer for another 15 minutes.

Meanwhile, heat oil in large skillet over medium-high heat. Add onions and peppers; cook 5 minutes or until just softened.

Add tomatoes, cinnamon, cardamom, cayenne, paprika and salt. Cover, reduce heat to low, and cook 7 minutes or until tender.

Stir vegetables into cooked lentils and simmer for 10 minutes to desired consistency.

Sprinkle with parsley.

MAKES 6 SERVINGS.

Per Serving:
calories 286
protein 16 g
carbohydrates 48 g
fat 6 g

Nutrient Highlights:
calcium 55 mg
iron 6 mg
zinc 2 mg

Beet & Cabbage Borscht

What can be said about borscht? It's filling and good for you. I have combined beets with cabbage, enjoyed the soup hot and cold ... and once prepared five hundred portions for a soup kitchen dinner cabaret!

PREPARATION TIME: 15 MINUTES
COOKING TIME: 30 MINUTES

2 tsp olive oil *10 mL*
1 onion, chopped
2 cups chopped red cabbage *500 mL*
1 tsp caraway seeds *5 mL*
6 cups vegetable stock *1.5 L*
8 beets, peeled and sliced (approx. 2 lb/1 kg)
¼ cup red wine vinegar *50 mL*
½ tsp salt *2 mL*
½ tsp pepper *2 mL*
¼ cup yogurt *50 mL*
2 Tbsp chopped chives *25 mL*

Heat oil in non-stick saucepan over medium-low heat. Add onion and cabbage; cover and cook 10 minutes or until tender, stirring occasionally. Add caraway seeds.

Add stock and beets and bring to a boil. Reduce heat and simmer, covered, about 30 minutes until beets are tender. Stir in vinegar, salt and pepper.

Purée beet mixture in food processor or blender until smooth.

Garnish each serving with a dollop of yogurt sprinkled with chives.

MAKES 8 SERVINGS.

Per Serving:
calories 112
protein 4 g
carbohydrates 20 g
fat 3 g

Nutrient Highlights:
calcium 55 mg
iron 2 mg

Garlic Soup with Potatoes & Cumin

I adore garlic. I use it all the time. I wanted to use 12 cloves in this soup, but my recipe taster, Kate, reminded me that not everyone enjoys garlic as much as I do. It's a good soup cold. Serve it with a toasted bagel and you have a delicious meal.

PREPARATION TIME: 35 MINUTES

6 cloves garlic, minced
1 Tbsp olive oil *15 mL*
2 tsp salt *10 mL*
2 bay leaves
2 Tbsp chopped fresh basil *25 mL*
½ tsp black pepper *2 mL*
6 cups water *1.5 L*
4 potatoes, thinly sliced
2 tsp cumin *10 mL*
2 egg yolks
2 oz Gruyère (or Old Cheddar) cheese, grated *75 g*

Place garlic, olive oil, salt, bay leaves, basil, pepper and water in a soup pot. Bring to boil; reduce heat and simmer for 20 minutes.

Remove bay leaves.

Add potatoes and cumin; simmer for 15 minutes. Make sure the potatoes are tender.

Beat egg yolks in a bowl. Whisk in ½ cup (125 mL) soup
broth. Gradually whisk in to pot and heat very gently.
Serve, sprinkling each bowl with grated cheese.

*TIP: To save egg whites for later use, place in a small bowl and
cover with plastic wrap. Will keep in refrigerator for up to 4 days.
Bring to room temperature before using.*

Per Serving:
calories 353
protein 12 g
carbohydrates 53 g
fat 11 g

Nutrient Highlights:
calcium 157 mg
iron 3 mg
zinc 2 mg

65

Miso Soup with Sea Vegetables

*My signature soup.... Don't gasp when you see the price of kombu;
you only need 4 small pieces. Buy a small amount loose-leaf,
rather than pre-packaged. We use three — count 'em — three types of
sea vegetables: arame, kombu and hijiki. We soak and drain the arame,
use the kombu to flavour our 6 cups of water. Then we discard the
kombu and add the hijiki to the soup stock and eat it later as part of
the soup. Buy the best miso — unpasteurized, organic bean and grain
type. Store miso in refrigerator. Never, ever, boil!
I often add leftover rice or pasta: it's a very adaptable soup.*

PREPARATION TIME: 30 MINUTES

¼ *cup* arame *3 g*
6 *cups* water *1.5 L*
4 pieces kombu, 6" (15 cm) each
1 onion, chopped
2 carrots, thinly sliced
½ red pepper, chopped
1 tsp grated gingerroot *5 mL*
2 Tbsp mirin or rice vinegar *25 mL*
½ *cup* hijiki *6 g*
⅓ *cup* barley miso *75 mL*
8 oz tofu, diced *250 g*
½ *cup* mushrooms, sliced *125 mL*
¼ *cup* chopped chives *50 mL*

Soak arame in 1 cup (250 mL) water for 15 minutes;
drain.

Combine 6 cups (1.5 L) water and kombu in large soup

66

pot. Heat slowly over medium heat for 20 minutes; do not let water boil.

Meanwhile, cook onion, carrots, red pepper in skillet in 3 Tbsp (45 mL) water for 5 minutes. Add arame and cook another 5 minutes until vegetables are soft.

Remove softened kombu from soup; add gingerroot, mirin and hijiki. Bring stock to a simmer.

Pour ½ cup (125 mL) of stock into small bowl; whisk in miso until well blended. Stir miso mixture back into soup pot.

Add tofu, mushrooms and vegetable mixture. Simmer 5 minutes.

Serve hot with chives sprinkled on top.

MAKES 6 SERVINGS.

Per Serving:
calories 77
protein 5 g
carbohydrates 10 g
fat 3 g

Nutrient Highlights:
calcium 63 mg
iron 3 mg

SALADS

SALADS

SALADS ARE EXCITING. They are made from many ingredients: grains, noodles, tofu, sea vegetables — even lettuce! Lentils, mushrooms and spinach add a new dimension to salad and taste best eaten with pita bread.

Salad marinades must use the best basic ingredients: vinegars, oils, herbs must all be at their peak. Many of the recipes included require time to marinate. Although in my cooking classes we eat the dish as soon as it is finished since we're either very hungry or have run out of time, many salads taste better the next day. *Overnight Tabbouleh,* for example, requires time since the bulgur is too crunchy to eat until it has marinated.

I add my kitchen leftovers to salads. If I add ½ cup of cooked brown rice, plus an extra grated carrot to my *Marinated Tofu Salad,* I get a whole new texture! Salads don't have to be rabbit food; with a little imagination and decent leftovers, they can be transformed.

. \|/ .

ABOUT QUINOA

Quinoa (pronounced keen-wa), is a rich and balanced source of vital nutrients. This hardy, delicious grain, unique in taste and texture, comes from the Andes mountains of South America where it has been grown for thousands of years. Quinoa was one of the three staple foods, along with corn and potatoes, of the Inca civilization. Quinoa contains more protein than any other grain: an average of 16.2% (compared with 7.5% for rice, 9.9% for millet and 14% for wheat). Some varieties of quinoa are over 20% protein. The protein found in quinoa is of an unusually high quality. It is a complete protein with an essential amino acid balance close to the ideal — similar to milk! Besides its unique protein, quinoa also provides starch, sugars, oil (high in lonoleic acid), fibre, minerals and vitamins.

Unlike many other food crops, quinoa thrives in areas with high altitudes and low rainfall, and can grow in poor, sandy soil. It survives in pockets of the South American Andes and has been transplanted to the Colorado Rockies. Its adaptability has allowed it to grow in the high mountains of Ecuador, Peru, Bolivia, southern Columbia and in northern Argentina and Chile. In the Altiplano region of Peru and Bolivia, where yearly rainfall may be as little as 4 inches, quinoa is the main food crop.

Quinoa seed is disk-shaped with a band around its middle, usually pale yellow in colour. An annual, this plant grows from 3 to 6 feet in height and, similar to millet, has seeds that form large clusters at the end of the stalk. These seeds are covered in saponin, an extremely bitter, resin-like substance. The saponin prevents insect and bird predation, eliminating the need for pesticides. In order for the seeds to be eaten, the saponin must be removed. Traditionally this has been done by hand, by scrubbing the quinoa in alkaline water.

Quinoa can be prepared in many ways: cooked in soup, made into flour for bread or pie crusts. The leaves may be eaten as a vegetable, the stalks burned for fuel and the saponin-filled water from rinsing the quinoa used as a shampoo. There is very little waste.

Quinoa Salad with Roasted Nuts

My friend Pat Fletcher, who was manager of a health food store at the time, phoned me up one day to tell me about this amazing grain that had just arrived. It cooked quickly and had a near perfect protein nutritional profile. Pat had a special on balsamic vinegar and tamari roasted almonds — and the rest is history!

PREPARATION TIME: 20 MINUTES
CHILLING TIME: 1 HOUR

1 cup quinoa, well rinsed *250 mL*
¼ cup balsamic vinegar *50 mL*
2 Tbsp mirin *25 mL*
¼ tsp salt *2 mL*
2 Tbsp chopped fresh dill *25 mL*
1 celery stalk, diagonally sliced
½ cup tamari roasted almonds *125 mL*

Bring 1 ¾ cups (425 mL) water to a boil in medium saucepan.

Add quinoa, reduce heat and simmer 10 to 15 minutes or until quinoa is tender and all of the water has been absorbed.

Combine balsamic vinegar, mirin, salt, dill, celery and quinoa in large bowl.

Marinate in refrigerator for 1 hour, covered. Add tamari roasted almonds before serving.

MAKES 4 SERVINGS.

Tip: Use ½ cup of any roasted nut — cashew, peanut or pistachio.

Per Serving:
calories 290
protein 9 g
carbohydrates 41 g
fat 10 g

Nutrient Highlights:
calcium 112 mg
iron 5 mg
zinc 2 mg

OVERNIGHT TABBOULEH

*Jim, my husband, has an old Frank Zappa album called Overnight
Sensation. This is my answer to Frank: Overnight Tabbouleh.
Traditionally, bulgur is soaked in boiling water. Using this recipe,
the bulgur can be soaked in cold water a day ahead of time.
Soaking the bulgur overnight allows the grains to be delicately seasoned
by the pungent flavours of the vinaigrette. Tabbouleh is ideal for
stuffing pita breads; it's the sort of salad to which one can
add many kinds of vegetables and beans.*

PREPARATION TIME: 20 MINUTES

CHILLING TIME: OVERNIGHT

¼ *cup* lemon juice *50 mL*
½ *cup* red wine vinegar *125 mL*
1 clove garlic, minced
2 tsp Dijon mustard *10 mL*
½ *tsp* ground cumin *2 mL*
¼ *tsp* freshly ground pepper *1 mL*
pinch salt
½ *cup* olive oil *125 mL*
1 ½ *cups* bulgur *375 mL*
4 green onions, sliced
2 tomatoes, chopped
1 cucumber peeled, seeded and diced
1 carrot, grated
¼ *cup* chopped fresh coriander *50 mL*

Whisk together lemon juice, vinegar, garlic, mustard,
cumin, pepper and salt in large bowl.

Gradually whisk in oil.

Stir in bulgur to coat. Wait until dressing is absorbed and
add 1 cup cold water, or enough to cover bulgur plus an inch
(2.5 cm).

76

Cover and refrigerate for 6 hours or overnight.
Before serving, toss with vegetables and coriander.

MAKES 6 SERVINGS.

Keeps 2 days in the refrigerator.

Per Serving:
calories 309
protein 5 g
carbohydrates 34 g
fat 19 g

Nutrient Highlights:
iron 1 mg
zinc 1 mg

Tabbouleh Kasha

My Aunt Jenny cooks the best kasha (buckwheat groats) in the world. When I told her she inspired me to use this grain in a salad, she put aside her reservations and tasted it — and agreed with me that it was delicious. Olives, corn and tomatoes add needed colour to this earth-toned essential food. Even friends who aren't buckwheat fans have to admit that this really is a festive dish. As an additional serving idea, try lining a pita with lettuce leaves and filling with tabbouleh kasha.

PREPARATION TIME: 25 MINUTES

1 cup kasha *250 mL*
½ tsp salt *2 mL*
4 green onions, chopped
¼ cup chopped parsley *50 mL*
2 Tbsp chopped fresh coriander *25 mL*
1 small carrot, grated
1 cup corn *250 mL*
2 cloves garlic, minced
⅓ cup lemon juice *75 mL*
1 Tbsp soy sauce *15 mL*
¼ cup extra virgin olive oil *50 mL*
1 large tomato, sliced in small wedges
¼ cup green olives, sliced *50 mL*

Toast kasha in dry skillet over medium heat, stirring constantly, until kasha turns amber and smells fragrant (about 5 minutes).

Bring 2 cups (500 mL) water to a boil, add toasted kasha and salt.

Cover, reduce heat and simmer for 10 minutes or until water is absorbed. Cool.

Combine green onions, parsley, coriander, carrot, corn.

Toss, and add to cooked kasha. Stir.

Whisk together garlic, lemon juice, soy sauce and olive oil. Pour over kasha mixture; stir together.

Garnish with tomato slices and sprinkle with olives.

Chill for 30 minutes. Serve on lettuce-lined platter.

MAKES 6 SERVINGS.

Per Serving:
calories 214
protein 5 g
carbohydrates 30 g
fat 10 g

Nutrient Highlights:
iron 1 mg

Lentil Daikon Salad

Daikon are long, greyish-white Japanese radishes with a peppery flavour. They complement the lentils very well — their earthy crunchiness rounds off a bite of cooked lentil.

PREPARATION TIME: 10 MINUTES
COOKING TIME: 25 MINUTES
MARINATING TIME: 30 MINUTES

1 cup dried lentils *250 mL*
2 cloves garlic, halved
¾ tsp hot sauce *3 mL*
2 cloves garlic, minced
¼ cup lime juice *50 mL*
3 Tbsp red wine vinegar *45 mL*
3 Tbsp olive oil *50 mL*
salt
freshly ground pepper
1 cup daikon, cut into matchsticks *250 mL*
2 tomatoes, finely chopped
2 carrots, grated
½ red onion, chopped
1 zucchini, thinly sliced
½ cup chopped fresh coriander *125 mL*
10 spinach leaves

Rinse lentils. Bring to a boil in 8 cups (2 L) water with halved garlic. Reduce heat and simmer, covered, for about 25 minutes or until tender. (Reserve cooking liquid for use as vegetable stock.)

Whisk together hot sauce, garlic, lime juice, vinegar and olive oil in bowl. Add salt and freshly ground pepper to taste.

Add lentils and let sit up to 30 minutes.

Toss in daikon, tomatoes, carrots, onion, half the zucchini and coriander.

Line platter with spinach leaves and border with remaining zucchini. Place salad on top.

MAKES 8 SERVINGS.

TIP: When testing lentils to see if they are done, make sure to try several, as they often don't cook evenly.

Per Serving:
calories 138
protein 6 g
carbohydrates 18 g
fat 6 g

Nutrient Highlights:
iron 2 mg

MARINATED MUSHROOMS

A recipe from the King Ranch Spa days. Thanks to Kate Gammal, who was determined to use the leftover liquid either as a cocktail or broth. The mushrooms can also be used as a tasty garnish in any green salad or lunch sandwich. Kate doesn't recommend them in martinis, but I have seen her nibble away, scotch in hand, as she prepares a moveable feast. This dish makes a perfect addition to any antipasto platter. Use as an accompaniment to a noodle salad served at a picnic.

PREPARATION TIME: 20 MINUTES

2 *Tbsp* olive oil *25 mL*
4 cloves garlic, minced
2 *Tbsp* fresh thyme, finely diced *25 mL*
2 *Tbsp* chopped fresh parsley *25 mL*
½ *tsp* peppercorns, crushed *2 mL*
½ *tsp* crushed whole coriander *2 mL*
½ *tsp* salt *2 mL*
½ *cup* sherry vinegar *125 mL*
½ *cup* water *125 mL*
2 *cups* small button mushrooms *500 mL*

Heat oil in saucepan over low heat. Add garlic and cook about 2 minutes, until fragrant.

Stir in thyme, parsley, peppercorns, coriander, salt, vinegar and water and bring to boil. Boil for 3 minutes.

Add mushrooms, reduce heat and simmer for 7 minutes. Allow mushrooms to cool in liquid. Serve with or without liquid.

MAKES 2 CUPS (500 ML).

Per ½ Cup Serving:
calories 80
protein 1 g
carbohydrates 5 g
fat 7 g

MARINATED TOFU SALAD

Many mistake the pieces of marinated tofu for feta cheese — they often tell me if they had known it was tofu, they never would have eaten it. But they did, and they enjoyed it. Add some salad greens and you have a delicious meal. It is important for the tofu to marinate for 30 minutes.

PREPARATION TIME: 45 MINUTES
MARINATING TIME: 1 HOUR

MARINADE:

¼ cup red wine vinegar 50 mL
3 Tbsp olive oil 45 mL
1 Tbsp lemon juice 15 mL
1 clove garlic, minced
1 tsp salt 5 mL
½ tsp dried marjoram 2 mL

SALAD:

8 oz firm tofu 250 g
4 asparagus stalks
1 cup broccoli florets 250 mL
1 carrot, thinly sliced
½ red onion, finely chopped
1 cup cooked chick-peas 250 mL

Press tofu for 15 minutes. (See page 129 for detailed instructions.) Cut into 1" (2.5 cm) cubes.

Whisk together vinegar, oil, lemon juice, garlic, salt and marjoram in large bowl. Add tofu to marinade and toss to coat; marinate tofu 30 minutes.

Snap ends of asparagus and steam until tender-crisp, about

4 minutes. Plunge in cold water to stop further cooking. Drain well and set aside.

Repeat with broccoli.

Stir vegetables into tofu and toss to coat, marinate 1 hour.

Serve on lettuce-lined platter.

MAKES 4 TO 6 SERVINGS.

Keeps up to 2 days covered in the refrigerator.

Per Serving:
calories 170
protein 7 g
carbohydrates 13 g
fat 11 g

Nutrient Highlights:
calcium 75 mg
iron 3 mg

THE BEST ROASTED PEPPERS

Roasted peppers can be used in many ways. Cut into thin strips, they can fill a sandwich, garnish a pizza, or become part of a salad. Choose peppers that are firm and have flat, even surfaces. When covered with a thin layer of olive oil, stored in a jar and refrigerated, these peppers will last up to 10 days.

PREPARATION TIME: 30 MINUTES

2 large red or yellow peppers
2 Tbsp extra virgin olive oil *25 mL*
2 cloves garlic, thinly sliced
2 Tbsp chopped fresh dill *25 mL*
2 tsp balsamic or red wine vinegar *10 mL*
¼ tsp freshly ground pepper *1 mL*

TO ROAST PEPPERS OVER A GAS BURNER:

Set peppers directly in the flame. Using long tongs, turn every few minutes so that entire surface is exposed to flame and skin is charred all over.

Set finished peppers in bowl; cover with plastic wrap. Let stand for 15 minutes or until cool enough to peel.

Working over a sieve in a bowl, carefully peel away charred skin with a knife. Save all of the juices that gather in the bottom of the bowl.

Halve and seed each pepper. Cut flesh into strips and add strips to the bowl with the juices.

Toss with olive oil, garlic, dill, vinegar and pepper. Store, covered in refrigerator.

To Roast Peppers in an Electric Oven:

Place peppers on baking sheet on top rack under preheated broiler. Turning often, broil for 12 minutes or until completely charred.

Follow above method.

MAKES 2 CUPS (500 mL).

Keeps up to 10 days in the refrigerator.

Per ½ Cup serving:
calories 83
protein 1 g
carbohydrates 6 g
fat 7 g

Broccoli with Roasted Peppers, Olives & Feta Cheese

This salad is so delicious that it will be eaten up within minutes of completion. I have never had leftovers. Even the olives are devoured. You can wash some lettuce and scoop some salad into the middle of a few leaves, stuff a pita with sprouts, and make a meal just by itself!

PREPARATION TIME: 20 MINUTES

1 large bunch broccoli
2 Tbsp olive oil *25 mL*
2 cloves garlic, thinly sliced *2*
⅓ cup olives, pitted and sliced *75 mL*
1 roasted pepper, diced
1 tsp dried marjoram *5 mL*
2 Tbsp chopped fresh dill *25 mL*
⅓ cup feta cheese, crumbled *75 mL*
2 Tbsp lemon juice *25 mL*
2 Tbsp toasted pumpkin seeds *25 mL*
pinch pepper

Cut broccoli into fairly large florets. Steam for 3 to 5 minutes, until tender-crisp. Rinse under cold water to stop cooking.

Heat oil with sliced garlic in large skillet. Remove garlic when browned and add steamed broccoli, olives, peppers, marjoram and dill. Cook until just heated through.

Sprinkle feta, lemon juice and pumpkin seeds over broccoli, and toss to coat. Add pepper to taste.

Serve warm or at room temperature.

MAKES 4 SERVINGS.

TIP: In summer months substitute 1 lb (500 g) asparagus for broccoli. Cut into 2" (5 cm) pieces and steam for 3 minutes.

Per Serving:
calories 192
protein 9 g
carbohydrates 15 g
fat 13 g

Nutrient Highlights:
calcium 195 mg
iron 3 mg
zinc 2 mg

SPINACH SALAD THAT
KIDS WILL EAT

My kids like to eat a spinach salad with scrambled tofu and eggs. The olive oil and red wine vinegar gently coat the leaves and the crunch is a good texture to balance against the slipperiness of the eggs and tofu. Organic spinach is especially gritty, so be sure to rinse it carefully twice. It's well worth the effort!

PREPARATION TIME: 20 MINUTES

1 bunch fresh spinach
½ lb mushrooms, thickly sliced *250 g*
1 cup farmer's cheese, grated *250 mL*
1 small red onion
½ cup olive oil *125 mL*
¼ cup red wine vinegar *50 mL*
½ tsp oregano *2 mL*
1 clove garlic, minced
¼ tsp salt *1 mL*
½ tsp pepper *2 mL*

Wash spinach leaves; trim off stems. Pat leaves dry in tea towel. Tear into bite-sized pieces.

Peel, quarter and thinly slice red onion.

Toss together spinach, mushrooms, cheese and onions in large bowl.

Whisk together oil, vinegar, oregano, garlic, salt and pepper. Pour dressing over salad.

Toss gently to coat spinach leaves.

MAKES 6 SERVINGS.

Per Serving:
calories 236
protein 7 g
carbohydrates 6 g
fat 22 g

Nutrient Highlights:
calcium 186 mg
iron 2 mg
zinc 1 mg

Sea Vegetable Salad

By the sea, by the sea, by the beautiful sea.... Arame grows close to the ocean's surface and is very clean. It does not need a thorough rising. (See Glossary of Ingredients, page 223.) It is rich in iron and calcium. The dressing is quite fragrant and can be used for green salads as well.

PREPARATION TIME: 20 MINUTES

SALAD:

½ *cup* dried arame *6 g*
1 beet, peeled and grated
1 carrot, grated
6 mushrooms, thinly sliced
1 small zucchini, thinly sliced
¼ *cup* alfalfa sprouts *50 mL*
2 *cups* leaf lettuce, shredded *500 mL*

DRESSING:

1 ripe avocado
1 clove garlic, minced
3 *Tbsp* lemon juice *45 mL*
1 Tbsp caraway seeds, toasted and crushed *15 mL*
¼ *tsp* sea salt *1 mL*
1 Tbsp chopped fresh dill *15 mL*
1 large tomato, quartered and seeded

Soak arame in 1 cup (250 mL) cold water for 15 minutes. Drain and chop.

Combine arame, beet, carrot, mushrooms, zucchini and sprouts in large bowl.

Place on lettuce-lined platter or toss lettuce in.

Purée avocado, garlic, lemon juice, caraway seeds, salt,
dill and tomato in food processor or blender until smooth.
Drizzle or toss salad with dressing.

MAKES 4 SERVINGS.

Per Serving:
calories 120
protein 3 g
carbohydrates 12 g
fat 8 g

Nutrient Highlights:
calcium 50 mg
iron 2 mg

HOT & SOUR BUCKWHEAT
NOODLE SALAD

*People often say to me "so where's the hot & sour?" The combination
of cayenne pepper (hot) and red wine vinegar (sour) gives this noodle
salad a vivid delicious flavour. Of course, using some tamari, gingerroot
and garlic rounds out the taste, and noodles taste great hot or cold. Soba
noodles are an undiscovered treasure.*
(See Soba Nori Rolls, page 188.)

PREPARATION TIME: 20 MINUTES

SALAD:

½ *cup* dried mushrooms *125 mL*
1 Tbsp tamari *15 mL*
½ *lb* buckwheat noodles (soba) *250 g*
(60% whole wheat, 40% buckwheat)
1 Tbsp toasted sesame oil *15 mL*
1 English cucumber
3 Tbsp chopped fresh coriander *45 mL*
1 bunch spinach, washed and dried
1 tomato, cut in wedges

DRESSING:

2 Tbsp sesame tahini or crunchy peanut butter *25 mL*
2 Tbsp tamari *25 mL*
¼ *cup* red wine vinegar *50 mL*
¼ *tsp* cayenne *1 mL*
2 Tbsp toasted sesame oil *25 mL*
1 Tbsp fresh gingerroot, minced *15 mL*
1 clove garlic, minced

Place dried mushrooms in small bowl and add boiling water to cover. Add tamari and stir. Let stand, covered, for about 15 minutes, while you prepare the rest of the salad.

Cook noodles in large pot of boiling water until al dente, about 5 minutes. Drain, rinse with cold water. Toss with oil in bowl.

When mushrooms are soft, drain and rinse thoroughly to remove grit. Squeeze out moisture. Cut off stems and discard. Cut caps into slivers.

Thinly slice one half of cucumber; dice remaining half.

Toss noodles with mushroom slivers, diced cucumbers, coriander and dressing.

Line bowl or platter with spinach leaves, sliced cucumber, and top with noodle mixture. Garnish with tomato wedges and serve.

For dressing, whisk ingredients together in bowl until combined, about 2 minutes.

MAKES 6 SERVINGS.

Per Serving:
calories 263
protein 9 g
carbohydrates 39 g
fat 11 g

Nutrient Highlights:
calcium 74 mg
iron 3 mg
zinc 3 mg

LIME QUINOA SALAD

Have quinoa, will travel! From Ecuador to Colorado to Alberta!
Quinoa resembles millet in appearance and texture. It has a very
interesting food history (see page 72) and I hope it becomes a
staple in your kitchen. This is my favourite recipe to demonstrate how to
use quinoa. Quinoa is a nutritional powerhouse, and so easy to
prepare. Make sure to rinse this grain for 5 minutes, using
your hand or a spoon to swish it around.

PREPARATION TIME: 20 MINUTES

1 cup quinoa, well rinsed *250 mL*
1 carrot, grated
½ red pepper, finely diced
½ *cup* finely diced English cucumber *125 mL*
2 green onions, finely chopped
¼ *cup* finely chopped fresh coriander *50 mL*
¼ *cup* lime juice *50 mL*
3 Tbsp toasted sesame oil *45 mL*
¼ *tsp* salt *1 mL*

Bring 2 cups (500 mL) water to a boil in saucepan. Add
quinoa; reduce heat and simmer 15 minutes, stirring occa-
sionally until grain is tender and water has been absorbed.
Mix vegetables with quinoa.
Whisk together lime juice, oil, salt and pepper to taste.
Toss with vegetables and quinoa.
Serve salad an hour later or refrigerate for up to 4 days.
Just remember to toss it before you serve!

MAKES 4 SERVINGS.

Keeps up to 4 days in the refrigerator.

Per Serving:
calories 287
protein 6 g
carbohydrates 40 g
fat 12 g

Nutrient Highlights:
calcium 75 mg
iron 4 mg
zinc 2 mg

TAHINI DRESSING

*This dressing can accompany many a veggie or tofu burger (see pages 158
and 136) or can be used as a dairy-free salad dressing. Tahini is such a
full-bodied ingredient — very filling and incredibly tasty.
Use also as a dip or spread.*

PREPARATION TIME: 10 MINUTES

1 cup tahini *250 mL*
⅓ cup lemon juice *75 mL*
¾ cup water *175 mL*
½ tsp ground cumin *2 mL*
2 tsp tamari *10 mL*
3 cloves garlic, minced
¼ cup minced fresh parsley or basil *50 mL*

Whisk together tahini and lemon juice in bowl.
Slowly whisk in water until tahini thins out.
Stir in cumin, tamari, garlic and parsley.

MAKES 1 CUP (250 mL).

Keeps 4 days covered in refrigerator.

Per 1 Tablespoon Serving:
calories 75
protein 2 g
carbohydrates 3 g
fat 7 g

Nutrient Highlights:
zinc 1 mg

Honey Mustard Dressing

This salad dressing is made with low-fat yogurt and can also be used as a spread. The honey rounds out the flavour without making the dressing too sweet. Use a good quality mustard and you can pour it on anything.

PREPARATION TIME: 10 MINUTES

½ *cup* low-fat yogurt *125 mL*
1 Tbsp honey *15 mL*
1 Tbsp Dijon mustard *15 mL*
1 Tbsp white wine vinegar *15 mL*
2 Tbsp green onions, thinly sliced *25 mL*
¼ *tsp* black pepper *1 mL*

Combine yogurt, honey, mustard, vinegar, green onions and pepper.
Stir with a fork until thoroughly blended.

MAKES ¾ CUPS (175 mL).

Keeps 3 days covered in refrigerator.

Per 1 Tablespoon Serving:
calories 13
protein 1 g
carbohydrates 2 g
fat - g

DILL GOAT CHEESE DRESSING

A perfect dressing to fill a celery cavity or a small zucchini boat.
Use as a salad dressing over greens, coleslaw or stray vegetables.

PREPARATION TIME: 5 MINUTES

2 oz goat cheese *75 g*
⅔ cup skim milk *150 mL*
1 tsp rice vinegar *5 mL*
1/2 clove garlic, minced
1 Tbsp chopped fresh dill *15 mL*
freshly ground black pepper

Combine cheese, milk, vinegar, garlic, dill and pepper to taste in blender. Blend until smooth.

MAKES 1 CUP (250 mL).

Keeps up to 2 days covered in refrigerator.

Per 1 Tablespoon Serving:
calories 13
protein 1 g
carbohydrates .5 g
fat .5 g

BEAN & GRAIN DISHES

BEAN & GRAIN DISHES

SHOULD WE EAT MORE BEANS AND GRAINS? Yes. They're what most people in the world eat. While the protein in both beans and grains is considered "incomplete," since they are deficient or lacking in one or more of the essential amino acids, pairing the two food groups gives us high quality protein equal to that of meat. Protein from beans contains very little saturated fat and no cholesterol. Whole grains provide B vitamins, iron, zinc, calcium and fibre. A natural combination!

Breakfast Refried Beans don't have to be eaten just at breakfast; try them any time of day. Use them as a layer in a casserole, stuffed in a burrito, frozen for later use or enjoyed immediately with some corn chips and salsa. Our *Buckwheat Potato Pancakes* can be eaten hot or cold. Another variation on this recipe is to prepare the cooked mixture in a loaf pan. Bake, slice and serve as mock meat loaf. Can cooked grains be used as pie crust? Absolutely. The "pie" crust in *Bean Pie with Millet Crust* is a crunchy, light crust that blends well with the spicy bean filling. Try it with other bean fillings.

Sushi rice is white rice that has rice vinegar and mirin added to its cooking water. It is very sticky, and is combined with vegetables to make thick and thin nori rolls in our *Picnic Nori Roll* recipe. Sushi is quick and simple to assemble. Remember that the nori tears easily, so you need to thinly slice your filling ingredients. This dish can be served as either a main course or as an appetizer.

Chili with sun-dried tomatoes and nuts? Times have changed. Our *Pot-Luck Chili* can also be made into a soup — just add more tomato purée. Serve with fresh bread. The

Basmati Herb Pilaf can accompany any main course; its delicate herb flavour will pair nicely with any soy or vegetable casserole. Our recipe for *Wild Rice with Pine Nuts* is delicious and very filling. Stuff it in a pita with sprouts for lunch.

ABOUT BEANS

My kids ask why beans make them gassy — especially after a pot-luck dinner. I tell them that the problem is that whoever prepared the bean dish didn't properly soak their beans.... You can buy beans in cans that have been packaged without salt, but for those who want to cook beans at home, here's the scoop: gas from eating beans is caused by a missing enzyme in our digestive system. This missing enzyme (alpha-glactosidase) breaks down the bean sugar raffinose. So, the gas we experience is caused by the undigested raffinose sugar.

What to do?

1. Start by eating small beans like adzuki, lentils and split peas.
2. Gradually increase the frequency of times you eat them.
3. To release a large portion of the raffinose sugar in the beans, bring the beans to a boil, remove them from the heat and let them soak for 6 hours. Rinse them thoroughly and cook them in fresh cold water.

REFERENCE GUIDE FOR COOKING BEANS

Bean (1 Cup)	Water	Cooking Time	Yield
adzuki	3 cups	45 minutes	3 cups
black beans	3 cups	1½ hours	2 cups
chick-peas	4 cups	3 hours	2 cups
Great Northern	3½ cups	2 hours	2 cups
kidney	3 cups	2 hours	2 cups
lentils	3 cups	45 minutes	2¼ cups
navy beans	3 cups	2½ hours	2 cups
pinto beans	3 cups	2½ hours	2 cups
soybeans	4 cups	3½ hours	2 cups
split peas	3 cups	45 minutes	2¼ cups

COOKING BEANS:

- Sort beans or peas. Throw away any rocks or foreign matter and any discoloured beans or peas.
- Rinse in cold water.
- Cover beans or peas with 4 times their volume of water. Bring to a boil. Remove from heat.
- Soak them for 6 hours.
- Discard the soaking water. Add fresh water. Bring to a boil. Lower heat and simmer, partially covered.
- Add water as needed to keep beans or peas covered. Do not add salt or other seasoning until beans are tender.

ABOUT GRAINS

The more I explore old cookbooks and recipes from around the world, and the more I listen to my aunts tell me about the foods they ate fifty years ago, the more apparent it becomes that grains have been a basic food in most cultures.

In Greek mythology, grain is associated with Persephone and Demeter. She gave the earth seven grains: wheat, rye, oats, barley, millet, rice and corn. I would like to add a few of my favourites: quinoa, buckwheat, spelt and wild rice

Hades, god of the underworld, kidnapped Demeter's daughter, Persephone. Grief-stricken, Demeter, goddess of agriculture, refused to let anything grow until her daughter was returned to her. The myth has it that Persephone was found, but because she had eaten three pomegranate seeds, she had to go back to the underworld for three months every year. For three months, then, Demeter mourns — and that is why we have winter.

My kids ask a lot of questions, especially when a new word is introduced. So, it was only a matter of time before they began asking me what a "grain" was. Grains are in fact the seeds and fruits of cereal grasses. They grow all over the world — from humid, hot climates to arid, cold mountainsides.

Whole grains take longer to prepare, but they are well worth the effort. Grains contain protein, fats, carbohydrates, fibre, vitamins and minerals. These are found in the four layers common to most grains:

    hull — protective outer coating
    bran — source of fibre and B vitamins
    germ — source of vitamins, minerals, proteins, oils
            and vitamin E
    endosperm — interior, starchy kernel

Because of the filling effects of the bulk dietary fibre, it is difficult to overeat starch when its source is whole grains.

STORING GRAINS:

Most grains are easy to store. Those that have been milled into flour will last several months on the shelf if kept cool and dry in an airtight container out of direct sunlight. Whole grains with their germ intact contain oils that will go rancid if not kept cool. The best way to keep whole grains is to freeze them in containers or tight sealing plastic bags. Label the bags or containers with the date of purchase. Grains can also be stored in the refrigerator for six months.

CLEANING GRAINS:

Grains must be carefully cleaned before cooking — keep an eye out for any foreign material.

• Measure out the amount you need.
• Pour the grain into a fine mesh strainer. Plunge the strainer up and down about eight times in a large bowl filled with cold water. Lift out the strainer; throw away the water.
• Fill a bowl with clean water again and repeat plunging several times until the water remains clear.
• Rinse the grains one last time under cold running water.
• Run your fingers through the grain and remove any foreign material.

MORE TIPS ON USING GRAINS:

• Use a heavy pot with a lid.
• Measure grains in a dry cup measure.
• If all the water has been absorbed but the grains are not yet thoroughly cooked, stir in a few tablespoons of boiling water. Cover and cook over low heat.
• If there is too much water after the grains are cooked, simply drain the water off.

See page 72 for more information about quinoa.

REFERENCE GUIDE FOR COOKING GRAINS

Grain (1 cup)	Water	Cooking Time	Yield
basmati rice, brown	2¼ cups	45 minutes	3 cups
basmati rice, white	1¾ cups	15 minutes	3 cups
brown rice	2 cups	45 minutes	3 cups
sushi rice	2 cups	20 minutes	2½ cups
wild rice	3 cups	1 hour	4 cups
buckwheat	2 cups	15 minutes	2½ cups
bulgur wheat	1½ cups	20 minutes	2½ cups
cracked wheat	2 cups	25 minutes	2⅓ cups
millet	3 cups	45 minutes	3½ cups
quinoa	2 cups	15 minutes	2½ cups
whole barley	3 cups	1½ hours	3½ cups

Breakfast Refried Beans

Pinto, kidney and black beans are grouped together because they can be used interchangeably. Use kombu instead of bay leaves; you don't need to remove them when cooking for 1 ½ hours. The kombu will add flavour, thicken and be easily digested. Use kombu in your scratch tomato sauces and soups. (See Miso Soup with Sea Vegetables, page 66.) You can eat the beans right away or store in the refrigerator for up to 3 days. To reheat, melt a little butter or oil in a frying pan. Add the beans and fry, stirring until the beans are hot. Use this mixture as a filling in omelettes, enchiladas, tostadas, burritos or crêpes. Refried beans freeze really well. Use an old-fashioned ice cube tray, fill ¾ full; add 2 Tbsp (25 mL) water, wait 24 hours. Then unmould, place frozen bean cubes in plastic bag. Don't forget to date it!

PREPARATION TIME: 2 HOURS

2 cups uncooked beans, rinsed, soaked 6 hours *500 mL*
3 pieces kombu, 6" (15 cm) each (cut in 4)
1 Tbsp ground cumin *15 mL*
pinch cayenne
½ *tsp* black pepper *2 mL*
½ *tsp* dried oregano *2 mL*
1 tsp dried basil *5 mL*
1 tsp dried dill *5 mL*
½ *tsp* salt *2 mL*
3 Tbsp safflower oil *45 mL*
2 onions, chopped
1 red pepper, thinly sliced
1 green pepper, thinly sliced
4 cloves garlic, minced

Bring 8 cups (2 L) water, beans and kombu to a boil. Reduce heat and simmer, partially covered, stirring and skimming occasionally. Cook for 1½ hours until beans are very soft.

Mix together cumin, cayenne, pepper, oregano, basil, dill and salt in a small bowl.

Heat oil in skillet over medium heat. Add onions, red and green peppers and garlic; cook for 5 minutes until soft. Reduce heat to low, add spices and salt, and cook 2 minutes more, stirring often.

Stir in beans and continue to cook over very low heat for 20 minutes until aromatic, stirring frequently.

MAKES 5 CUPS (1.25 L).

Keeps up to 3 days in the refrigerator.
TIP: If using as a dip, mash beans while cooking.

Per Serving:
calories 346
protein 18 g
carbohydrates 51 g
fat 9 g

Nutrient Highlights:
calcium 91 mg
iron 6 mg
zinc 2 mg

BUCKWHEAT POTATO PANCAKES

*I grew up force-fed kasha, alias buckwheat groats. When you
combine sweet potatoes, green onions and almond nut butter,
the taste changes magically and those lowly groats are
uplifted into a sensational burst of flavour.*

PREPARATION TIME: 45 MINUTES

1 ½ cups kasha (buckwheat groats) *375 mL*
1 tsp sea salt *5 mL*
1 large onion, finely chopped
4 Tbsp toasted sesame oil *60 mL*
1 celery stalk, finely chopped
1 large carrot, grated
2 medium sweet potatoes, cubed
¼ cup almond butter or tahini *50 mL*
¼ cup chopped fresh basil *50 mL*
2 green onions, finely chopped
2 Tbsp soy sauce *25 mL*

Dry-roast kasha in a heavy skillet over medium heat for
5 minutes, stirring often with wooden spoon.

Add 3 cups (750 mL) water and salt. Cover and cook
over low heat until water is absorbed and kasha is tender,
about 15 minutes.

Cook onion in 1 Tbsp (15 mL) of the oil over medium
heat until softened. Add celery and carrot; cook for another
5 minutes until softened.

Steam or boil sweet potatoes 5 minutes, until tender;
drain and mash.

Stir together kasha, vegetables, almond butter, basil, green
onions and soy sauce until combined. Cool in refrigerator for
10 minutes.

Keeping hands moist, form into sixteen 2-inch patties. Heat remaining 3 Tbsp oil (45 mL) in large frying pan over medium-high heat. Cook patties 5 minutes, turning once, until golden brown and crisp.

MAKES 16 PANCAKES.

Per Serving:
calories 133
protein 3 g
carbohydrates 18 g
fat 6 g

Nutrient Highlights:
calcium 52 mg

Bean Pie with Millet Crust

My friend Doug Williams tested this recipe for me and told me it was "absolutely perfect." He is an accomplished cook. (He still hasn't given me his recipe for oven-roasted vegetable terrine!) Millet is a tasty grain and makes a firm crust. You could use other types of bean than pinto.... I often eat this first thing in the morning. Then coffee.

PREPARATION TIME: 20 MINUTES
COOKING TIME: 30 MINUTES

CRUST:

1 cup millet, well rinsed *250 mL*
1 egg, lightly beaten
2 Tbsp canola oil *25 mL*
½ tsp salt *2 mL*
1 Tbsp sesame seeds *15 mL*

FILLING:

2 cups cooked pinto beans *500 mL*
1 egg, or 3 oz/90 g puréed tofu
2 Tbsp ground cumin *25 mL*
¼ cup chopped fresh basil *50 mL*
1 tsp chili powder *5 mL*
¼ cup good-tasting nutritional yeast *50 mL*

TOPPING:

2 tomatoes, thinly sliced
1 cup grated Monterey Jack cheese *250 mL*

Preheat oven to 400°F (200°C).
Bring 3 cups (750 mL) water to a boil; stir in millet.
Reduce heat and cook, covered, for 20 minutes, until tender.

Mix together cooked millet, egg, oil, salt and sesame seeds. Press mixture into a greased 9" x 13" (3.5 L) baking dish, covering bottom and halfway up the sides.

Bake crust for 12 minutes, until lightly golden. Reduce heat to 350°F (180°C).

Blend together beans, egg, cumin, 2 Tbsp (25 mL) of the basil, chili powder and yeast in food processor or blender until smooth.

Fill crust with bean mixture and arrange sliced tomatoes on top. Sprinkle with remaining basil and top with grated cheese.

Bake for 30 minutes, until cheese is bubbling.

MAKES 6 SERVINGS.

Per Serving:
calories 417
protein 19 g
carbohydrates 53 g
fat 15 g

Nutrient Highlights:
vitamin B 123 mcg
calcium 227 mg
zinc 3 mg

Pot-Luck Chili

Many food magazines are heralding a return to traditional foods,
or "comfort foods." When I read about these foods, I mentally change
ingredients until they are low in fat, organic where possible,
and easy to prepare. One popular recipe making a big splash is
old-fashioned chili. I have introduced sea vegetables, sun-dried
tomatoes, organic vinegars and lots of fresh herbs.
Add more tomato purée to use as a soup.

PREPARATION TIME: 30 MINUTES
COOKING TIME: 1½ HOURS

1 ½ lbs   dried pinto or kidney beans   *750 g*
4 tsp   safflower oil   *20 mL*
2   onions, chopped
8   cloves garlic, minced
3   pieces kombu
1 Tbsp   ground cumin   *15 mL*
½ tsp   cayenne pepper   *2 mL*
1 Tbsp   paprika   *15 mL*
2 Tbsp   chili powder   *25 mL*
2 tsp   dried basil or oregano   *10 mL*
1 tsp   salt   *5 mL*
1   red pepper, seeded and diced
1   green pepper, seeded and diced
16   sun-dried tomatoes, sliced
1   can (28 oz/784 g) tomatoes
2 Tbsp   apple cider vinegar   *25 mL*
½ cup   chopped fresh basil   *125 mL*
1 cup   roasted cashews   *250 mL*

Soak beans for 6 hours. Drain and rinse carefully, check-
ing for rocks or alien beans.

Heat 2 tsp (10 mL) of the oil over medium heat in large stockpot. Sauté 1 onion with 4 cloves garlic for 5 minutes, or until soft.

Add beans, 10 cups (2.5 L) water and kombu. Bring to a boil. Reduce heat to low, cover, and simmer, skimming and stirring occasionally for 1¼ hours, until beans are tender.

Toast ground cumin in dry skillet, stirring for 3 minutes or until aromatic. Remove from heat. Stir in cayenne, paprika, chili powder, basil and salt.

In a second stockpot, heat remaining oil and cook remaining onion, 3 of the garlic cloves, and peppers for 5 minutes.

Add spices and sun-dried tomatoes. Continue cooking, stirring for 5 minutes. Add water if necessary to prevent spices from sticking.

Add canned tomatoes, breaking up with back of spoon. Bring to a simmer; cover and simmer over low heat for 25 minutes, stirring often.

Stir in beans with liquid. Add remaining garlic clove. Continue simmering for 1 hour, covered, stirring frequently.

Add vinegar, basil and cashews just before serving.

Serve with pita, cornbread, or bagels.

MAKES 10 SERVINGS.

TIP: 1 ½ lbs (750 g) dried beans = three 19 fl oz (540 mL) cans beans.

Per Serving:
calories 316
protein 17 g
carbohydrates 49 g
fat 8 g

Nutrient Highlights:
calcium 128 mg
iron 7 mg
zinc 3 mg

Basmati Herb Pilaf

*The pilaf method is to first fry the rice, then add the water and herbs.
This rice dish can be used in a variety of ways to create a complete
meal — it can easily be stuffed inside a pita with a few pieces
of marinated tofu, or served with a kebob.*

PREPARATION TIME: 10 MINUTES
COOKING TIME: 40 MINUTES

3 Tbsp safflower oil *45 mL*
1 cup uncooked basmati rice, rinsed *250 mL*
2 onions, chopped
2 cloves garlic, minced
2 Tbsp finely chopped fresh basil *25 mL*
2 Tbsp finely chopped fresh parsley or coriander *25 mL*
1 tsp sea salt *5 mL*
½ tsp freshly ground black pepper *2 mL*

Heat oil in medium-sized pot over medium heat. Add
rice, onions and garlic. Cook for 5 minutes, stirring often,
until onions are softened.

Stir in 2½ cups (625 mL) water, basil, parsley, salt and
pepper; mix together.

Bring to boil, then reduce heat and simmer, covered, for
40 minutes or until the water is absorbed. Check rice after 30
minutes; if there is a lot of water left, remove cover and finish cooking. If rice looks dry, add a little more water.

Let cooked rice sit in pot, covered, for 15 minutes before
serving. This allows the grains of rice to firm up so they stay
separate and don't clump together.

MAKES 4 SERVINGS.

Per Serving:
calories 280
protein 4 g
carbohydrates 42 g
fat 11 g

Nutrient Highlights:
iron 3 mg

WILD RICE WITH PINE NUTS

*The sauté smell will fill the house with aromas beyond your imagina-
tion. A fragrant, chewy salad that I like to serve with melon. I shape
the rice into a ring on a round platter and place bite-size chunks of
cantaloupe and honeydew in the centre. My four year old daughter
Mackenzie wants to wear the rice ring around her noble brow —
a festive wreath, she says. I have used this filling for cabbage rolls,
but that recipe will be in the next book....*

PREPARATION TIME: 45 MINUTES
CHILLING TIME: 1 HOUR

1 cup organic wild rice *250 mL*
1 cup brown rice *250 mL*
½ tsp salt *2 mL*
¼ cup olive oil *50 mL*
¼ cup lemon juice *50 mL*
3 Tbsp canola oil *45 mL*
2 Tbsp cider vinegar *25 mL*
2 cups mushrooms, sliced *500 mL*
4 cloves garlic, minced
2 celery stalks, diced
½ red pepper, diced
½ cup roasted pine nuts *125 mL*
2 Tbsp chopped fresh parsley *25 mL*

Wash wild and brown rice.

Bring 4½ cups (1.125 L) water to a boil. Stir in rice and
salt. Cover, reduce heat and simmer for 45 to 55 minutes or
until just tender.

When cooked, combine wild and brown rice in bowl and
set aside to cool. As rice cools, add olive oil and lemon juice
to prevent the rice sticking.

Combine canola oil, vinegar and mushrooms in small bowl. Allow to marinate for at least 1 hour.

Heat skillet over medium heat. Add marinated mushrooms (along with any marinade that hasn't been absorbed) and minced garlic. Cook until mushrooms are just tender, about 3 minutes.

Stir celery, red pepper and pine nuts into rice; mix well. Allow to finish cooling in refrigerator at least 1 hour. Serve on a bed of leaf lettuce.

MAKES 10 SERVINGS.

TIP: Moulds well into individually shaped servings or as a ring.

Per Serving:
calories 258
protein 6 g
carbohydrates 32 g
fat 13 g

Nutrient Highlights:
iron 2 mg
zinc 2 mg

SOY DISHES

Soy Dishes

IS THE "DAIRY CASE" at your local natural food store in transition? In addition to the usual food items (milk, eggs and cheese), are the shelves lined with cartons of soy milk, packages of tempeh and miso, and cartons of tofu? Many of these foods are beginning to ape their conventional counterparts, and so we are being offered "soy hotdogs," "tofu baloney" and soy-based "ice creams." The ads for these new food items imply that they are better for your health, but as you would with any food purchase, make sure you read the labels and compare prices.

Soy foods are nutritious. Studies indicate that, per acre, soybean crops provide fifteen times more protein than animal sources. Soy foods are rich in calcium, iron, B vitamins and vitamin E. They are inexpensive, both ecologically as well as economically. One acre of land used to grow soy will provide the protein requirements for an individual for 2,000 days. Soybeans grow close to the ground, are highly pest-resistant, use less water than cattle and add nitrogen to the soil. Soy foods are easy and versatile to prepare. They can be interchanged for the meat ingredient in many main dishes. Soy milk and cheese are lactose-free alternatives to cow or goat milk for use on cereal or in desserts.

Be forewarned: raw tofu is eaten only by Buddhist monks in Sixties-type recipe books! Tofu has no flavour — that is why we marinate it and combine it with other more flavourful ingredients. Toddlers might eat small portions of raw tofu (I recall my son Cameron not knowing better), but if you are over the age of two, and especially if this is your first tofu adventure, don't taste it until it has been properly marinated!

Tempeh must never be eaten raw. Due to the presence of a live bacterial culture (which is why it is called a "cultured" soy product), it must be cooked: either stir-fried, oven-roasted or steamed. Tempeh is made by splitting the soybeans, cooking them, removing the hulls and incubating the beans. Tempeh should be white with a few dark grey spots. It is usually sold frozen. Steaming tempeh for fifteen minutes before marinating or adding it to a recipe allows it to absorb flavour more easily.

· ✳ ·

About Soy Sauce

Soy sauce is made by soaking and cooking soybeans. These are then mixed with cracked roasted wheat and inoculated with a culture called koji. When the culture has covered the wheat and soy, it is mixed with sea salt and water, placed in huge wooden barrels, and allowed to ferment slowly for two and a half years. The mixture is then strained to remove the soy and wheat meal. Oil is skimmed from the surface and the remains are then pasteurized and bottled. Good quality soy sauces are the equivalent in their epicurean value of fine, well matured wines.

ABOUT MISO

Miso is a Japanese word, but the pressing of fermenting soy-beans to make a soybean paste was learned from the Chinese. This process was further developed by the Japanese to suit their own taste much in the way various cultures developed various national cheeses. Miso is pervasive in Japanese cooking and can be used in soups, gravies, sauces, stir-frying and as a marinade, a pickling medium, as a stock, in stews, salad dressings and drinks. To make miso, the soybeans are soaked and steamed, and the cereal (rice, barley, buckwheat) is also cooked. These are mixed together and a yeast culture is then added. The culture takes four days to grow throughout the mixture. After it has spread, sea salt is added and the mixture is placed in huge cedar vats. A lid is placed on the vats and stones piled onto the lid to create immense pressure. Depending on the time of year, the proportions and the style of the miso, the mix is then fermented, untouched, for from three months to three years.

Each miso has its own distinct flavour, colour and aroma. Like yogurt, unpasteurized miso is also abundant in lactic acid bacteria and enzymes, which aid in food digestion. Sweet miso is usually light in colour (yellow or beige) and high in carbohydrates. It is marketed as mellow miso, finger lickin' good miso, and white miso. Because it is high in koji and low in salt, sweet miso ferments in two to eight weeks.

Miso with a higher salt content, lower koji content and proportionately more soybeans is darker in colour and saltier in taste than sweet light miso. It must be fermented for a longer period of time, two to three years. This type of miso is marketed as rice miso, brown rice miso and barley miso.

ABOUT TOFU

Tofu, soybean curd, soy cheese — this off-white cake has many identities and none of them ever suggests, in taste or appearance, its soybean source. Tofu's custard-like consistency is reminiscent of cottage cheese, yet it is not a dairy product and not a cheese.

What exactly is tofu? Traditionally, *tofu* meant a fresh soybean slurry curdled from whole soybeans. They were soaked, ground, mixed with water, heated, filtered, coagulated and formed into blocks.

Because of its remarkable versatility, high protein and low fat content, tofu will become of increasing importance in the Western diet. It blends easily into many different cuisines from spicy mid-Eastern dishes to the subtle flavours of Mediterranean cooking to the fiery piquancy of South American classics. While Western cooks are still learning to meld tofu's adaptable nature to their favourite cuisine, the Eastern world enjoys this staple in many traditional ways.

Nowadays, tofu is sold in several ways: in bulk packed in water, in plastic tubs and in vacuum packages. The pre-packaged containers will list the ingredients — soybeans, water, coagulating agent (calcium sulfate, nigari, magnesium chloride, Epsom salts, lemon juice or vinegar) — as well as the nutritional information (fat, protein and calories) and the expiry or best-before date.

Tofu that you buy as loose pieces or in plastic tubs should be immersed in water in a tightly closed container and refrigerated. It should be used within a week to ten days from when it was bought. To insure maximum freshness, change the water of stored tofu every day, if possible, and at least every other day. Although the tofu you buy in plastic tubs is already in water, you should remove it from the container when you get home and store it in fresh water in a closed container. Vacuum-packed tofu need not be opened and stored in water. It will keep for about a month if unopened. Once opened, it should be stored in the same way as loose tofu and used within ten days.

If you find yourself with leftover tofu approaching the expiry date, freeze it. Freezing affects the structure to such an extent that frozen tofu becomes an entirely different ingredient. Whereas fresh tofu is dense and tender, frozen tofu is chewy, with an open, coarse texture resembling veal or chicken. Freezing also increases tofu's sponge-like ability to absorb the flavours of any cooking medium.

Tofu will freeze faster if you cut the cakes into halves or thirds. Wrap each piece of tofu in plastic wrap, then seal in plastic bags. This individual packaging will allow you to remove pieces as desired. Use frozen tofu within six months.

Frozen tofu must be defrosted before using. Remove all plastic wrap and place tofu in a deep bowl. Cover with boiling water. Let stand for ten minutes and drain. When thawed, rinse with cool water, then press firmly between your palms to expel all moisture. The defrosted tofu should be as dry as possible. Frozen tofu's highly absorbent quality is useful in dishes which require marinating or cooking in sauces and stews. Its chewy texture makes it more attractive than regular tofu to meat-eaters. It thaws quickly too.

PRESSING TOFU

Why do we press tofu? To reduce its water content and make it more absorbent so that it can more readily take on flavours from marinades. Pressed tofu is my favourite take-along on a picnic salad. It can easily be tossed and will not crumble, and can masquerade as feta cheese. Serve with pita bread or on its own — it's a winner!

To press, slice your cake of tofu in half. The slices should be of uniform thickness so that the tofu will press evenly.

Select two plates of the same size. Place two layers of white napkins or paper towelling on the bottom plate. Place the slices of tofu on top of the napkins, then another layer of napkins on top of the tofu. Place the second plate on top.

Select a suitable 5 lb (2 kilo) weight. (I use the base of my food processor.) Place weight on top of plate.

Press for 30 minutes, near sink for easy draining.

TOFU MAYONNAISE

*The best tofu mayonnaise this side of a soybean — this recipe makes a
perfect accompaniment to many of the dishes which follow. The flavour
of the mustard and red wine vinegar blend well with tofu — a nice
light taste when you want a dash of mayonnaise. I once prepared a
large batch of tofu mayonnaise that I used to make two hundred
sandwiches of various fillings — and everyone commented on
how tasty the dressing was. A good introduction to tofu!*

PREPARATION TIME: 10 MINUTES

8 oz tofu 250 g
1/2 cup yogurt 125 mL
3 Tbsp lemon juice 45 mL
2 Tbsp red wine vinegar 25 mL
1 Tbsp safflower oil 15 mL
1 clove garlic, minced
2 tsp tamari 10 mL
1 1/2 tsp Dijon mustard 7 mL
pinch freshly ground black pepper

Purée tofu in blender or food processor until smooth.
Add yogurt, lemon juice, vinegar, oil, garlic, tamari, mustard and pepper. Blend until smooth.

MAKES 1½ CUPS (375 ML).

Keeps 1 week covered in the refrigerator.
TIP: For a dairy-free mayonnaise, substitute
¼ cup (50 mL) water for yogurt.

Per 1 Tablespoon Serving:
calories 16
protein 1 g
carbohydrates 1 g
fat 1 g

ROUX-SOY

A hearty, stick-to-your-ribs casserole. This is one of my most popular frozen dinners. Though it was known as Bean Grain Casserole, it deserves a more worthy name. It is now possible to buy cooked soybeans in a can from your health food store. What a treasure!

PREPARATION TIME: 25 MINUTES
COOKING TIME: 1 HOUR

1 cup bulgur *250 mL*
2 cups cooked soybeans *500 mL*
2 Tbsp butter *25 mL*
1 tsp paprika *5 mL*
1 tsp ground cumin *5 mL*
1 tsp cinnamon *5 mL*
2 Tbsp sunflower seeds *25 mL*
2 Tbsp shredded coconut *25 mL*
2 Tbsp raisins *25 mL*
3 green peppers, chopped
2 onions, chopped
2 cloves garlic, minced
2 tomatoes, chopped
3 Tbsp tomato paste *50 mL*

SAUCE:

3 Tbsp butter *45 mL*
¼ cup whole wheat flour *50 mL*
2 cups milk *500 mL*
¼ cup chopped fresh parsley *50 mL*
2 Tbsp wheat germ *25 mL*
¼ cup Parmesan cheese *50 mL*

Preheat oven to 350°F (180°C).

Place bulgur in bowl and cover with 1¼ cups (300 mL) boiling water; let sit covered for 15 minutes until water has been absorbed.

Purée beans in food processor or blender with 1 cup (250 mL) water until smooth; combine with bulgur.

Melt butter in skillet on low heat; stir in paprika, cumin, cinnamon, sunflower seeds, coconut and raisins. Increase heat to medium and stir in green peppers, onions and garlic. Continue to cook for 5 minutes, or until softened.

Stir in tomatoes and tomato paste and continue cooking for 7 minutes.

Combine vegetables with bulgur mixture and spread into greased 9" x 13" (3.5 L) baking dish.

Meanwhile, melt butter in small pot over low heat. Whisk in flour and cook for 3 minutes, whisking constantly. Gradually whisk in milk and bring to boil. Cook, whisking constantly, for 5 minutes or until thickened. Stir in parsley.

Pour sauce over casserole and sprinkle with wheat germ and Parmesan.

Bake for 45 minutes, covered with tin foil. Uncover and cook 15 more minutes.

MAKES 6 SERVINGS.

Per Serving:
calories 428
protein 21 g
carbohydrates 47 g
fat 20 g

Nutrient Highlights:
calcium 254 mg
iron 6 mg
zinc 3 mg

TOFU STROGANOFF

What a great dish to introduce people to tofu! The tofu absorbs the delicious taste of the marinade, and everything is further enhanced with the addition of sautéed onions and mushrooms. (Use a combination of button, shiitake and oyster mushrooms.) Served with noodles or rice, this recipe will guarantee raves all round.

PREPARATION TIME: 30 MINUTES
MARINATING TIME: 1 HOUR

2 *lb* tofu, pressed for ½ hour *1 kg*
½ *cup* tamari *125 mL*
½ *cup* water *125 mL*
3 *Tbsp* olive oil *45 mL*
3 *Tbsp* lemon juice *45 mL*
3 cloves garlic, minced
¼ *cup* mirin or white wine *50 mL*
2 *Tbsp* ketchup *25 mL*
2 *tsp* minced fresh gingerroot *10 mL*
2 *Tbsp* olive oil *25 mL*
2 onions, chopped
2 *cups* chopped mushrooms *500 mL*

Preheat oven to 350°F (180°C).

See page 129 for instructions on how to press tofu. Slice tofu into 1" x 1½" x ¼" (2.5 cm x 4 cm x .5 cm) thick pieces. Place in single layer in 13" x 9" (3.5 L) baking dish.

Combine tamari, water, 3 Tbsp (45 mL) of the olive oil, lemon juice, garlic, mirin, ketchup and gingerroot in saucepan. Heat over medium heat; pour over tofu. Marinate for 1 hour.

Heat 2 Tbsp (25 mL) olive oil in large skillet over medium heat. Cook onions, stirring for 5 minutes, or until soft. Add mushrooms; cook for another 5 minutes, stirring until golden and moisture has evaporated.

Spoon mushroom mixture over marinated tofu mixture. Bake in preheated oven for 30 minutes or until heated through.

MAKES 6 SERVINGS.

TIP: Leftovers are great for using as a cabbage roll filling or pita stuffing.

Per Serving:
calories 272
protein 15 g
carbohydrates 14 g
fat 19 g

Nutrient Highlights:
calcium 180 mg
iron 10 mg
zinc 2 mg

TOFU BURGERS

*When I outline my cooking course, informing my students that one
evening will be devoted to tofu, I hear a collective groan from one end
of the room to the other that culminates in a definitive question:
Will it be tasty? At that point, everyone unburdens themselves of a
failed tofu experience, usually involving a tofu burger.
These burgers are very tasty. Allow a few minutes for sautéed
ingredients to cool down before you start forming burgers,
mixing into tofu mixture, and let stand. Serve on rolls or bread with
lettuce, pickles, sprouts and Tofu Mayonnaise (see page 131).
See page 129 for detailed instructions on pressing tofu.*

PREPARATION TIME: 20 MINUTES
COOKING TIME: 15 MINUTES

1 lb tofu, pressed for ½ hour *500 g*
¼ cup nut butter *50 mL*
1 Tbsp safflower oil *15 mL*
1 onion, sliced
2 Tbsp chopped fresh basil *25 mL*
1 cup thinly sliced mushrooms *250 mL*
1 cup grated carrot *250 mL*
½ cup ground sunflower seeds *125 mL*
1 cup bread crumbs *250 mL*
2 Tbsp tamari *25 mL*
pinch freshly ground black pepper

Preheat oven to 350°F (180°C).

Purée tofu in food processor or blender; add nut butter
and continue puréeing until smooth.

Heat oil in skillet over medium heat; cook onion with
basil for 7 minutes or until lightly browned.

Add mushrooms and carrot; cook for 5 minutes more. Stir into tofu mixture.

Mix in sunflower seeds, ½ cup of the bread crumbs, tamari and pepper.

Using ¼ cup mixture per patty, form into patties. The recipe can be made up to this point up to 4 hours ahead. Coat patties with remaining bread crumbs.

Bake on parchment paper-lined baking sheet in preheated oven for 15 minutes, turning once until browned and heated through.

MAKES 10 BURGERS.

Per Burger:
calories 182
protein 8 g
carbohydrates 14 g
fat 11 g

Nutrient Highlights:
calcium 93 mg
iron 4 mg
zinc 1 mg

Curried Tofu in Pita Bread

Use fresh curry powder; it should be less than 6 months old. Line each pita with ¼ cup (50 mL) alfalfa sprouts — they serve as a crunchy layer — and stuff the pita with this delicious curry tofu vegetable mixture. Or cook some rice and serve side by side.

PREPARATION TIME: 25 MINUTES

3 *Tbsp* canola oil *45 mL*
2 onions, sliced
2 *cups* sliced mushrooms (button, shiitake, oyster) *500 mL*
1 carrot, grated
2 *cups* thinly sliced cabbage *500 mL*
3 *Tbsp* whole wheat pastry flour *45 mL*
2 *tsp* curry powder *10 mL*
1 *cup* soy milk *250 mL*
8 *oz* puréed tofu *250 g*
¾ *tsp* salt *3 mL*
¼ *tsp* pepper *1 mL*
6 4" (10 cm) round pita breads
1 ½ *cups* alfalfa sprouts *375 mL*

Heat 1 Tbsp (15 mL) of the canola oil in large frying pan on medium-high heat. Cook onions for 5 minutes, or until softened.

Add mushrooms, carrot and cabbage and cook 8 minutes more, stirring often.

Meanwhile, heat remaining oil in saucepan over medium heat. Whisk in flour and curry powder and cook 2 minutes, or until lightly browned

Whisk in soy milk gradually. Bring to a boil, reduce heat and cook, whisking, for another 5 minutes, or until thickened.

Mix in tofu and cook just long enough to heat through, about 2 minutes. Add salt and pepper.

Mix tofu curry sauce and vegetables in a large bowl.

Cut top off pitas. Heat in 350°F (180°C) oven for 3 minutes, until heated.

Stuff each pita with an equal amount of curried tofu mixture.

MAKES 6 SERVINGS.

Per Serving:
calories 311
protein 13 g
carbohydrates 44 g
fat 11 g

Nutrient Highlights:
calcium 120 mg
iron 5 mg
zinc 1 mg

ABOUT TEMPEH

Tempeh is a delicious, perfect protein made from soybeans. It has been a staple in Indonesian cooking for hundreds of years and is today very popular in the West. Tempeh can be used as a main course, in sandwiches, dips, salads and soups.

Tempeh is a cake of cooked soybeans bound together by a white mycelium, much in the same way as Camembert or Brie. Like yogurt, tempeh is a cultured food. It is made by the controlled fermentation of soybeans. The friendly spore culture, *rhizospirus oligosporus,* is mixed with the partially cooked soybeans. The beans are spread out in flat sheets about one-half inch thick and incubated at 88°F (31°C) for twenty-eight to thirty-two hours. The beans are then bound by the mould into firm cakes.

The fermentation process does much more than bind the beans together however. It enhances the flavour, and enzymes from the mould break down the complex proteins, fats and carbohydrates of the soybeans, making them easier to digest and assimilate. In addition to making regular soybean tempeh, the beans are often combined with grains such as rice, millet and barley before inoculation and incubation.

Choose tempeh in which the beans are tightly bound together by a dense white mycelial growth. Black or grey spots are the result of natural sporulation of the mould and not an indicator of spoilage.

Fresh or defrosted tempeh will keep five days in a refrigerator and six months in a freezer; it must be thoroughly cooked before eating.

There are many ways to cook this versatile food, so here are a few tasty ideas:

Steam — slice in half; steam for 15 minutes.
Microwave — 7 minutes.
Precook in broth — 10 minutes.
Pan fry — heat oil; thinly slice tempeh; sauté on both sides until reddish brown, 8 minutes.
Bake in oven — see recipe for *Oven-Roasted Tempeh & Vegetables*, page 146.

Once cooked, tempeh can be placed in the refrigerator for four more days and leftovers can be refrozen. Tempeh will thaw in the refrigerator within eight hours, outside the refrigerator in five hours.

TEMPEH SLOPPY JOES

I dare anyone to guess what this recipe is made from! Serve with rice, on top of a pizza, stuffed in cabbage rolls, pita, over whole wheat buns or a grain of your choice ... the possibilities are endless! If you don't have fresh or frozen vegetable stock available, I would recommend Morga or Hügli vegetable cubes.

PREPARATION TIME: 25 MINUTES

½ cup safflower oil *125 mL*
20 oz tempeh, thawed and crumbled *600 g*
1 large onion, chopped
2 cloves garlic, minced
5 ½ oz can tomato paste *156 mL*
2 cups vegetable stock *500 mL*
¼ cup red wine vinegar *50 mL*
¼ cup Barbados molasses *50 mL*
2 Tbsp tamari *25 mL*
2 tsp mustard *10 mL*
2 tsp chili powder *10 mL*

Heat oil in wok or frying pan, reserving 2 tsp (10 mL). Sauté tempeh for 12 minutes or until reddish brown. Drain on paper towel.

Cook onion and garlic in medium pot in remaining oil for 5 minutes or until softened over medium heat. Add tomato paste, stock, vinegar, molasses, tamari and mustard. Simmer for 10 minutes. Add chili powder and tempeh. Simmer for 5 minutes more.

MAKES 6 SERVINGS.

Per Serving:
calories 328
protein 17 g
carbohydrates 20 g
fat 23 g

Nutrient Highlights:
iron 6 mg
zinc 1 mg

TEMPEH REUBEN

*My friend and colleague Marilyn Crowley has a teenage son, Matthew,
who is a vegetarian. Matthew will demolish three of these Tempeh
Reubens in one sitting. He doesn't always use the tofu mayonnaise as a
spread, but needs both hands to hold the sandwich together.*

PREPARATION TIME: 20 MINUTES

8 oz tempeh *250 g*
2 Tbsp canola oil *25 mL*
2 Tbsp soy sauce *25 mL*
6 slices rye bread
6 slices Swiss cheese
2 small tomatoes, sliced
1 small red onion, sliced in rings
lettuce leaves and sprouts

SPREAD:

½ cup Tofu Mayonnaise (see page 131) *125 mL*
¼ cup ketchup *50 mL*
1 Tbsp chopped fresh dill or 1 tsp (5 mL) dried *15 mL*
1 tsp Dijon mustard *5 mL*
1 Tbsp chopped chives *15 mL*

Preheat oven to 400°F (200°C).

Slice tempeh into thirds crosswise; with knife parallel to
counter, slice pieces in half to make 6 pieces.

Mix together oil and soy sauce in large bowl. Toss with
tempeh to coat.

Bake on lightly greased or parchment-paper lined baking
sheet for 15 minutes, or until reddish brown.

Meanwhile, lightly toast bread with cheese until cheese is

melted. Cover one slice with spread and garnish with tempeh, tomato, onion, lettuce and sprouts.

MAKES 3 SERVINGS.

TIP: Use leftover spread for dip with vegetables.

Per Serving:
calories 618
protein 39 g
carbohydrates 42 g
fat 36 g

Nutrient Highlights:
iron 9 mg
zinc 4 mg

Oven-Roasted Tempeh
& Vegetables

A warm, satisfying stew that resembles a goulash. The flavours of tahini and rosemary leave a rich taste in the mouth. Oven-roasting the tempeh allows us to cut back on the amount of oil normally used. Tempeh can be sliced crouton sized and will evenly absorb the marinade and will brown. Serve with rice or pasta.

PREPARATION TIME: 1 HOUR 15 MINUTES

3 Tbsp soy sauce *45 mL*
¾ cup water *175 mL*
¼ cup olive oil *50 mL*
¾ lb tempeh, cut into ¼ inch (.6 cm) cubes *375 g*
2 Tbsp sesame seeds *25 mL*
6 cloves garlic, minced
2 onions, chopped
4 medium sweet potatoes, cut in ½ inch (1.25 cm) cubes
2 carrots, cut in ½ inch (1.25 cm) pieces
¾ lb celeriac, cut into ½ inch (1.25 cm) cubes *375 g*
3 celery stalks, cut into ½ inch (1.25 cm) lengths

SAUCE:

2 Tbsp olive oil *25 mL*
¼ cup soy sauce *50 mL*
¼ cup white unbleached flour *50 mL*
¼ cup good-tasting nutritional yeast *50 mL*
1/4 cup tahini *50 mL*
¼ cup chopped fresh basil *50 mL*
1 tsp dried rosemary *5 mL*
½ tsp black pepper *2 mL*
2 cups water *500 mL*

146

Preheat oven to 350°F (180°C).

Combine soy sauce, water and 2 Tbsp (25 mL) of the olive oil in bowl. Stir in tempeh and let sit 5 minutes. Sprinkle with sesame seeds.

Bake on lightly greased or parchment paper-lined baking sheet for 10 minutes. Remove and set aside.

Heat remaining oil in pot over medium heat. Cook garlic and onions for 5 minutes or until softened.

Transfer to 13" x 9" (3.5 L) baking dish. Add sweet potatoes, carrots, celeriac, celery and baked tempeh.

To make sauce, heat 2 Tbsp (25 mL) olive oil in same pot over medium heat. Whisk in soy sauce, flour, yeast, tahini, basil, rosemary and pepper. Cook until thickened, about 2 minutes. Very gradually whisk in water. Cook, whisking constantly until thickened.

Pour sauce over vegetables and tempeh.

Bake, covered, for 50 minutes, stirring twice, until tender. Add more water if necessary.

Stir and serve.

MAKES 6 SERVINGS.

Per Serving:
calories 483
protein 21 g
carbohydrates 44 g
fat 28 g

Nutrient Highlights:
vitamin B12 2.5 mcg
zinc 3 mg

POTATO & TEMPEH PATTIES

They look just like latkes; the good-tasting nutritional yeast gives them a reddish glow that attracts the eye. Serve with a leafy green salad and slices of raw vegetables and you have one tasty meal. No sampling the uncooked tempeh, though; it must always be cooked, never eaten raw.

PREPARATION TIME: 25 MINUTES

4 medium potatoes, cubed
2 sweet potatoes, cubed
8 oz tempeh *250 g*
1 tsp salt *5 mL*
1 tsp ground cumin *5 mL*
1 tsp ground coriander *5 mL*
¼ tsp cayenne pepper *1 mL*
3 cloves garlic, minced
5 egg whites
½ cup good-tasting nutritional yeast *125 mL*
2 Tbsp canola oil *25 mL*

Steam potatoes for 5 minutes, until tender. Mash in blender or food processor. Crumble tempeh into potatoes and mash. Add salt, cumin, coriander, cayenne and garlic. Purée until slightly chunky.

Using wet hands, form mixture into twelve 3" by ½" (7.5 cm x 1.25 cm) patties.

Whisk together egg whites in shallow bowl. Place yeast in separate bowl. Dip patties in egg whites and coat in yeast.

Heat oil in skillet over medium heat. Working in batches, fry patties 10 minutes, turning once until reddish brown. Add oil as necessary.

MAKES 12 PATTIES.

Per Patty:
calories 154
protein 9 g
carbohydrates 25 g
fat 3 g

Nutrient Highlights:
vitamin B12 2.5 mcg
zinc 1 mg

MOSTLY VEGGIES

MOSTLY VEGGIES

TOO OFTEN PEOPLE ASSUME that vegetarians eat exclusively vegetables, unaware that grains, beans and soy foods make up a significant part of our diet ... so it is with reluctant pride that we call this chapter "Mostly Veggies."

Our *Nut Loaf or Burgers*, so dense and chewy, are best right out of the oven. Mix and match your mushrooms in our *Provençal Mushroom Stew*. *Goat Cheese Spinach Casserole* is a favourite from my cooking course — layers of grain, greens, sautéed veggies and goat and cottage cheese. It is topped off with grated cheese, tomatoes and pumpkin seeds: a server's dream.

Our *Tempeh Paella with Artichokes & Seitan* recipe is an introduction to seitan or wheat meat. The basic ingredient in seitan, which is eaten all over the world, is a high gluten wheat flour (check for specific ingredients on the label). Seitan is traditionally cooked with tamari, ginger, garlic and water. It is also sold in jars and in an instant form. Combining seitan with tempeh and sea vegetables gives an unbelievable earthy taste to the food. I often serve my Paella with angel hair pasta or brown rice.

Moussaka is a Greek dish using lamb, eggplant and mushrooms topped by a béchamel sauce (made with egg yolks and cream). Imagine the challenge of creating a low-fat vegetarian version of this traditional dish! In our light *Vegetarian Moussaka* the mushroom sauce is so flavourful, the baked eggplant so delicious, that meat-eaters are convinced there must be meat in this mixture! This is perfect holiday food served with some steamed vegetables — carrots and broccoli — and a green salad.

For our *Ratatouille* recipe, we bake instead of frying the ingredients in large amounts of oil. *Thai Broccoli* gets a lot of its flavour from the use of a jalapeño pepper. Curry powder is a combination of many spices — up to seventy. Most packaged curry powders contain fifteen different spices. In our *Spinach-Zucchini Curry* recipe we use seven. Get out the spice grinder! You may want to toast the cumin seeds in this recipe before grinding them. Nice aroma. Serve with *Cucumber Raita*, especially if you're just getting used to hot foods. Raita, a yogurt prepared dip, will calm down excited taste buds.

When I'm cubing the vegetables for *Vegetable Shish Kebab*, I always prepare an extra few since they sometimes crumble or get eaten before they reach the skewer! If you end up with any leftover tofu or potato cubes, add them to a salad or bake in the oven for 10 minutes, basted once, at 300°F (150°C).

ABOUT NORI

Nori, made for over 300 years from the red algae cultivated in Japan's bays and inlets, is the most popular of sea vegetables. In its uncultivated form, nori is closely related to laver, which grows wild on ocean granite beds. It is nori, not the wild laver, that is used for the civilized thin sheets so often used in sushi making. Nori is harvested in the colder months, sun-dried on bamboo mats, then pressed into sheets.

Available in health food stores wrapped in cellophane packages, nori comes in deep purplish or olive-brown sheets. It is also available in the form of sushi nori, already toasted.

Of all the varieties of commercially distributed sea vegetables, it is hard to match nori in nutritional value. At 35% protein, nori is the richest sea vegetable in high quality protein. It is also rich in vitamin A. High in vitamin C, the B vitamins, calcium, magnesium, potassium and phosphorous, nori also contains enzymes that are believed to aid digestion.

Unlike most other sea vegetables, nori is never reconstituted. It is used toasted. To prepare nori that has not been pre-toasted, use tongs to hold one sheet at a time about 7" to 8" (15 to 17 cm) away from a medium flame on your stove. Toast just until the nori turns a bright olive green.

To use as a garnish for noodles, miso broth and rice dishes, cut toasted nori into fine strips (½" x 2"/1.25 x 5 cm or so) or simply crumble or tear it. Add one or two sheets of crumbled nori, rice vinegar, a touch of honey and minced scallions and serve as a side dish.

PICNIC NORI ROLLS

*Every summer we vacation at a laid-back cottage that is part of a
group of cottages called Billie Bear. One day the kids were bored
with making cookies, so we were looking for a new cooking activity.
We found a few sushi mats that hadn't yet been exposed to
play-dough ... and the kids had a ball. Vegetarian sushi is ideal for a
picnic. It travels well, is dairy-free and so simple to prepare. Easy to
make with a sushi mat, nori rolls can be filled with a variety of
steamed or raw vegetables and seasonings. To make perfect rolls, use
fresh warm rice, and ensure that all surfaces and ingredients are dry —
any excess moisture will soften the nori and it might tear.
Delicious as a main course or as an appetizer.*

PREPARATION TIME: 20 MINUTES
COOKING TIME: 20 MINUTES

1 cup sushi rice *250 mL*
2 Tbsp mirin *25 mL*
1 Tbsp rice vinegar *15 mL*
¼ tsp salt *1 mL*
4 sheets nori
1 ripe avocado
2 Tbsp lemon juice *25 mL*
2 tsp Dijon mustard *10 mL*
½ tsp wasabi powder *2 mL*
4 green onions, trimmed to same length as nori sheets
5 sun-dried tomatoes, softened and cut into strips

DIPPING SAUCE:

2 Tbsp soy sauce *25 mL*
1 tsp wasabi powder *5 mL*
¼ cup water *50 mL*

Rinse rice well in a strainer till water runs clear. Bring 2 cups (500 mL) water to boil in medium pot; add rice, mirin, vinegar and salt. Return to boil. Cover and simmer on low heat for 20 minutes or until liquid is absorbed. Don't stir rice.

Let rice stand until cool enough to handle.

Using tongs, toast nori sheets over hot burner for a minute, waving sheets back and forth. Nori should change colour slightly and become crisp.

Peel avocado and cut into thin slices. Sprinkle with 1 Tbsp (15 mL) of the lemon juice.

Mix mustard, wasabi and 1 tsp (5 mL) water in small bowl to make a paste.

Place one nori sheet (shiny side down) on sushi mat, with long end facing you.

Spoon ½ cup (125 mL) warm rice onto nori sheet. Press rice firmly with spatula to cover sheet. Leave a 1" (2.5 cm) strip of nori uncovered along top. About 1" (2.5 cm) from bottom of nori sheet, spread ½ tsp (2 mL) mustard paste. Place green onion strip on mustard, then place 2 slices of avocado on top (overlapping if necessary). Add a few thin strips of sun-dried tomato.

To roll, lift sushi mat (at the edge closest to you) and begin to roll up, holding the filling in place with index fingers. Roll nori, neatly and firmly, like a jelly roll, almost to the end. Using finger tip, moisten top strip of nori with some of remaining lemon juice to seal the roll. Fill and roll remaining nori. Cut each roll into 5 pieces.

Mix soy sauce, wasabi and water in small bowl to make dipping sauce.

MAKES 20 PIECES.

Per Serving:
calories 56
protein 1 g
carbohydrates 9 g
fat 2 g

Nut Loaf or Burgers

Preparation of this recipe is not really time consuming if you have a food processor to aid in the grating of all the vegetables. If you prefer to grate manually, go right ahead. This recipe is low calorie, with a small amount of cooking fat. It can be baked as a loaf or divided into 9 patties and baked in the oven. Either way the recipe provides an enjoyable alternative to burgers and meat loaves.

PREPARATION TIME: 40 MINUTES

1 Tbsp canola oil *15 mL*
4 cloves garlic, minced
1 ½ cups thinly sliced onion *375 mL*
1 carrot, grated
1 celery stalk, grated
1 zucchini, grated
1 cup grated daikon *250 mL*
1 cup grated yellow squash *250 mL*
1 cup grated mushrooms *250 mL*
¼ cup soy sauce *50 mL*
½ tsp black pepper *2 mL*
1 Tbsp chopped fresh Italian parsley *15 mL*
¼ tsp dried oregano *1 mL*
1 tsp dried thyme *5 mL*
1 tsp dried dill *5 mL*
1 cup sesame seeds *250 mL*
1 cup pecans or almonds *250 mL*
½ cup dried bread crumbs *125 mL*

Preheat oven to 400°F (200°C).

Heat oil in large skillet over medium heat. Cook garlic and onions 5 minutes, until softened. Add carrot, celery, zucchini, daikon, yellow squash and mushrooms and cook 20 minutes, stirring occasionally, until liquid has evaporated. Add soy sauce, pepper, parsley, oregano, thyme and dill.

Place sesame seeds and pecans in food processor and pulverize. Add nut mixture to vegetables and mix well.

Form mixture into 9 oval patties, about 3" (7.5 cm) long. Roll patties in bread crumbs, place on lightly greased cookie sheets and bake for 10 minutes or until patties are lightly browned.

Alternatively, lightly grease 8" x 4" (1.5 L) loaf pan. Sprinkle with 2 Tbsp (25 mL) bread crumbs and bake in 350°F (180°C) oven for 15 minutes. Garnish with extra parsley.

MAKES 6 SERVINGS.

Per Serving:
calories 355
protein 12 g
carbohydrates 24 g
fat 26 g

Nutrient Highlights:
calcium 340 mg
iron 6 mg
zinc 3 mg

PROVENÇAL MUSHROOM STEW

*This rich, filling main course is best served with croutons or large
pieces of fresh crusty bread. Mix your mushrooms — button, shiitake,
portobello, oyster — and you will have a very tasty, satisfying meal.
See page 58 for* Vegetable Stock *recipe.*

PREPARATION TIME: 45 MINUTES

¼ cup canola oil *60 mL*
2 onions, chopped
4 cloves garlic, minced
3 carrots, chopped
4 celery stalks, chopped
2 red peppers, chopped
5 cups vegetable stock *1.25 L*
1 cup red wine or mirin *250 mL*
4 potatoes, cubed
2 tsp dried thyme *10 mL*
2 tsp dried marjoram *10 mL*
1 tsp salt *5 mL*
¼ tsp cayenne *1 mL*
½ tsp black pepper *1 mL*
8 Tbsp canola oil *120 mL*
8 Tbsp flour *120 mL*
¼ cup tomato paste *60 mL*
3 Tbsp canola oil *45 mL*
1 ½ lb mushrooms, thickly sliced *750 g*

Heat ¼ cup (60 mL) of the canola oil in skillet over
medium heat. Cook onion, garlic, carrots, celery and red
pepper for 12 minutes, until softened.

Combine stock, wine, vegetables, potatoes, thyme, marjoram, salt, cayenne and pepper in large pot. Bring to boil; cover, reduce heat and simmer.

Meanwhile in small pot, heat 8 Tbsp (120 mL) canola oil. Whisk in flour and cook 3 minutes. Whisk in 2 cups (500 mL) stew liquid and tomato paste. Return to stew and simmer until thickened, about 5 minutes.

Heat remaining 3 Tbsp (45 mL) of the canola oil in skillet over medium-high heat. Cook mushrooms for 5 minutes, until browned. Add to stew and simmer until potatoes are tender, about 15 minutes.

MAKES 10 SERVINGS.

Per Serving:
calories 250
protein 5 g
carbohydrates 30 g
fat 10 g

Nutrient Highlights:
iron 3 mg
zinc 1 mg

Goat Cheese Spinach Casserole

Tofu meets goat cheese meets Swiss chard. Or egg meets cottage cheese meets spinach. A versatile recipe with distinct layers that hold together well. An excellent dish to serve to non-believers.

PREPARATION TIME: 25 MINUTES
COOKING TIME: 40 MINUTES

1 cup bulgur *250 mL*
2 eggs or 8 oz (250g) tofu, puréed
4 oz goat cheese *125 g*
1 cup cottage cheese *250 mL*
¼ *cup* good-tasting nutritional yeast *50 mL*
½ *cup* chopped fresh basil *125 mL*
¼ *cup* tomato paste *50 mL*
1 Tbsp red wine vinegar *15 mL*
3 Tbsp safflower oil *50 mL*
2 onions, sliced
4 cloves garlic, minced
2 zucchini, thinly sliced
½ *tsp* dried oregano *2 mL*
1 tsp dried marjoram *5 mL*
1 tsp black pepper *5 mL*
1 lb spinach or Swiss chard,
washed and finely chopped *500 g*
¼ *cup* grated Monterey Jack or Cheddar cheese *50 mL*
2 tomatoes, thinly sliced
¼ *cup* toasted pumpkin seeds or sesame seeds *50 mL*

Preheat oven to 350°F (180°C).

Place bulgur in bowl and pour over 1¼ cups (300 mL) boiling water. Cover and let sit 15 minutes or until water has been absorbed.

Meanwhile, lightly beat eggs in medium bowl. Mix in goat cheese, cottage cheese, yeast, basil, tomato paste and vinegar. Using fork, stir mixture into bulgur until thoroughly combined.

Heat oil in skillet over medium-high heat. Cook onions and garlic about 5 minutes, or until soft. Add zucchini, oregano, marjoram and pepper. Cook 8 minutes more, or until zucchini is tender.

Assemble in a greased 9" x 13" (3.5 L) casserole dish. Layer bulgur mixture first, spinach next, then sautéed vegetables and, at last, goat and cottage cheese mixture. Top with grated Monterey Jack, tomato slices and seeds.

Bake covered in preheated oven for 30 minutes. Uncover and bake another 10 minutes. Allow to stand 5 minutes before serving.

MAKES 6 SERVINGS.

Per Serving:
calories 350
protein 21 g
carbohydrates 37 g
fat 15 g

Nutrient Highlights:
vitamin B12 2.6 mcg
calcium 280 mg
iron 3 mg

TEMPEH PAELLA WITH
ARTICHOKES & SEITAN

My Portuguese girlfriend Gabriella grew up eating paella. She thinks this dish is simply delicious — and recognizes the capers. Paella is a Spanish seafood dish. I have appropriated the name for this meal. When you combine oven-roasted tempeh, seitan, arame with coloured peppers, olives and tomatoes, you have a fantastic splash of tasty foods that invite you to DIG IN.

PREPARATION TIME: 50 MINUTES

6 *Tbsp* olive oil *85 mL*
1 *Tbsp* soy sauce *15 mL*
1/4 cup water *50 mL*
1 lb tempeh, cut into ¼" (.6 cm) cubes *500 g*
1 *Tbsp* sesame seeds *15 mL*
1 onion, sliced into ¼" (.6 cm) crescents
3 cloves garlic, minced
1 red pepper, cut into ¼" (.6 cm) strips
1 yellow pepper, cut into ¼" (.6 cm) strips
4 celery stalks, sliced
2 *large* tomatoes, cut into wedges
2 tsp sea salt *10 mL*
1 can (6 fl. oz./170 g) can artichoke hearts
½ *cup* pitted olives, thinly sliced *125 mL*
3 *Tbsp* olive juice *45 mL*
¾ *cup* arame *175 mL*
2 *Tbsp* capers *25 mL*
2 *Tbsp* caper liquid *25 mL*
½ *lb* seitan, cut into strips *250 g*

164

1 tsp chili powder *5 mL*
1 tsp hot sauce *5 mL*
1 tsp black pepper *5 mL*

Preheat oven to 350°F (180°C)

Combine 4 Tbsp (45 mL) of the olive oil, soy sauce and water in bowl. Stir in tempeh and let sit 5 minutes. Sprinkle with sesame seeds. Pour tempeh and mixture onto baking sheets.

Bake on lightly greased or parchment-paper lined baking sheets for 10 minutes. Remove and set aside.

Heat remaining oil in large pot over medium heat. Add onion and garlic; cook 5 minutes or until softened. Add peppers and celery. Cook 5 minutes, or until softened. Add tomatoes, 1 tsp (5 mL) of the sea salt and artichoke hearts. Cover and cook for 8 minutes, stirring occasionally.

Stir in olives, olive juice, arame, capers, caper liquid, seitan, remaining 1 tsp (5 mL) salt, chili powder, hot sauce, pepper and baked tempeh. Simmer uncovered for 15 minutes.

MAKES 6 SERVINGS.

Per Serving:
calories 394
protein 23 g
carbohydrates 21 g
fat 27 g

Nutrient Highlights:
calcium 145 mg
iron 6 mg
zinc 1 mg

VEGETARIAN MOUSSAKA

When I was selling frozen vegetarian dinners, this was my number one, all-time best seller. This moussaka is sensuous. I love to inhale the fragrant aroma of eggplant and mushroom baked to perfection with a tasty white sauce. This is the meal to serve to those who can't imagine a meal without meat.

PREPARATION TIME: 40 MINUTES

COOKING TIME: 35 MINUTES

3 eggplants, sliced ½" (1.25 cm) thick
2 Tbsp olive oil *25 mL*
3 cloves garlic, minced
1 onion, chopped
12 cups sliced mushrooms (about 2 lbs/1 Kg) *3 L*
1 5½ oz (156 mL) can tomato paste
¼ cup chopped fresh basil *50 mL*
1 tsp soy sauce or salt *5 mL*
¼ cup dry red wine or mirin *50 mL*
½ cup good-tasting nutritional yeast *125 mL*
¼ cup butter *50 mL*
¼ cup whole wheat pastry flour *50 mL*
1 ¼ cups milk or soy milk *300 mL*
½ cup freshly grated Parmesan cheese *125 mL*
½ tsp salt *2 mL*
¼ tsp pepper *1 mL*
pinch nutmeg

Preheat oven to 350°F (180°C).

Place eggplant on lightly greased or parchment paper-lined baking sheet. Bake for 20 minutes, turning once, until browned.

Heat oil in large pot over medium heat. Cook garlic and onion for 5 minutes or until softened. Increase heat to medium-high and stir in mushrooms in batches of 2 cups (500 mL) at a time, making sure they are softened before adding next batch.

Reduce heat to medium, stir in tomato paste, basil, soy sauce, wine and yeast. Simmer for 5 minutes or until sauce is thickened.

Melt butter in small pot over medium heat. Whisk in flour and cook until thickened, about 2 minutes. Very gradually, whisk in milk. Cook, whisking constantly, until thickened, about 5 minutes. Stir in Parmesan, salt, pepper and nutmeg.

Place one layer of eggplant in lightly greased 13" x 9"(3.5 L) baking dish. Cover with mushroom sauce and spread cheese sauce smoothly on top.

Bake, covered, for 20 minutes. Continue baking uncovered for another 15 minutes until golden.

MAKES 6 SERVINGS.

TIP: Moussaka can be assembled, covered and refrigerated up to 12 hours ahead. Bring to room temperature and bake.

Per Serving:
calories 378
protein 20 g
carbohydrates 45 g
fat 17 g

Nutrient Highlights:
vitamin B12 5 mcg
calcium 282 mg
zinc 5 mg

RATATOUILLE

*Delicious hot or cold, this is a basic vegetarian recipe. I have tried to
cut back on the amount of oil used and bake the stew using herbs
and condiments for flavour. Serve with pasta or
open-faced on a fresh Italian roll.*

PREPARATION TIME: 45 MINUTES
COOKING TIME: 30 MINUTES

1 small eggplant, cubed
1 tsp salt *5 mL*
3 Tbsp olive oil *45 mL*
2 cloves garlic, minced
1 red onion, thinly sliced
1 green pepper, seeded, thinly sliced
1 tsp fennel seeds *5 mL*
1 tsp chopped fresh rosemary *5 mL*
2 tsp chopped fresh thyme *10 mL*
¼ cup mirin *50 mL*
4 tomatoes, coarsely chopped
2 Tbsp tomato paste *25 mL*
pinch salt
½ tsp pepper *2 mL*
1 zucchini, thinly sliced
2 tomatoes, thinly sliced
¼ cup freshly grated Parmesan cheese *50 mL*
¼ cup pecans, sliced *50 mL*

Preheat oven to 350°F (180°C). Lightly oil oval shallow
oven-proof dish.

Place cubed eggplant on lightly greased or parchment-
paper lined baking sheet. Bake for 20 minutes.

Meanwhile, heat 1 Tbsp (15 mL) of the olive oil in large skillet over medium heat. Cook garlic, onion, green pepper, fennel seeds, rosemary and thyme for 5 minutes.

Add baked eggplant to skillet with mirin, tomatoes, tomato paste, salt and pepper. Simmer over medium heat for 10 minutes or until mixture is thick and most of the liquid has evaporated.

Transfer vegetables to prepared dish. Arrange alternating circles of zucchini and tomato slices over the top and drizzle zucchini with remaining oil. Bake for 30 minutes.

Mix cheese and pecans. Sprinkle on top along with extra fresh herbs — rosemary and thyme. Bake for a further 15 minutes, until golden.

MAKES 6 SERVINGS.

Per Serving:
calories 184
protein 5 g
carbohydrates 19 g
fat 11 g

Nutrient Highlights:
calcium 92 mg
iron 2 mg

THAI BROCCOLI

An exciting new way to serve broccoli and use up your leftover tofu. Serve hot or cold. Love those trees! See page 129 for instructions on pressing tofu.

<small>PREPARATION TIME: 30 MINUTES</small>

¾ *cup* hot vegetable stock or water *175 mL*
1 stalk lemongrass, trimmed, finely chopped
2 bunches broccoli
2 Tbsp toasted sesame oil *25 mL*
3 cloves garlic, minced
1 jalapeño pepper, seeded and finely chopped
½ *lb* firm tofu, cut into ½" (1.25 cm) cubes *250 g*
1 small red pepper, cut into ¼" x 1" (.5 cm x 2.5 cm)
strips
½ *cup* finely chopped fresh coriander *125 mL*
1 Tbsp lime juice *15 mL*
4 green onions, halved and cut into ½" (1.25 cm) slices
2 Tbsp soy sauce *25 mL*

Pour stock over lemongrass in small bowl. Let steep while you are preparing broccoli.

Cut broccoli into small florets. Peel stalks and cut into ½" (1.25 cm) slices.

Heat oil over medium-high heat in wok or large skillet. Add garlic, jalapeño and tofu. Stir-fry for 1 minute. Add broccoli, red pepper and lemongrass/stock mixture. Cover and cook over medium heat for 5 minutes.

Stir in coriander, lime juice, green onions and soy sauce. Cover and cook until broccoli is tender-crisp, about 2 minutes.

MAKES 4 SERVINGS.

Per Serving:
calories 186
protein 12 g
carbohydrates 16 g
fat 11 g

Nutrient Highlights:
calcium 164 mg
iron 5 mg
zinc 1 mg

Spinach-Zucchini Curry

Get out the seasoned wok! You can use a combination of sweet and regular potatoes. I leave the skins on because they are organic. We are making our own curry powder in this recipe, combining our own spices. To increase the heat, use more cayenne. This dish has a wonderful aroma, and I often serve it with basmati rice and raita. It is delicious cold as well. Makes a good meal on the go.

PREPARATION TIME: 30 MINUTES

1 lb organic potatoes *500 g*
1 lb green beans, trimmed and
cut into 1" (2.5 cm) pieces *500 g*
1 zucchini, thickly sliced
¼ cup butter *50 mL*
5 onions, thickly sliced
5 cloves garlic, minced
2 tsp ground turmeric *10 mL*
1 Tbsp ground coriander *15 mL*
1 Tbsp ground cumin *15 mL*
½ tsp paprika *2 mL*
½ tsp cayenne *2 mL*
½ tsp black pepper *2 mL*
¼ tsp cinnamon *1 mL*
1 bunch spinach, coarsely chopped
2 green chilies, finely chopped
2 Tbsp lime juice *25 mL*
2 Tbsp grated fresh gingerroot *25 mL*
¾ cup water *175 mL*

Scrub potatoes, quarter lengthwise and slice thickly. Boil with green beans in salted water for 5 minutes; drain and set aside.

172

Boil zucchini for 3 minutes; drain and set aside.

Melt butter in large pot over medium heat. Cook onions and garlic for 5 minutes until onions begin to colour. Add turmeric, coriander, cumin, paprika, cayenne, pepper and cinnamon, stirring for a few minutes until aromatic.

Stir in potatoes, green beans, zucchini and spinach; then add chilies, lime juice, gingerroot and water. Simmer for 10 minutes, stirring frequently, until most of the water is absorbed and vegetables are tender. Serve with *Cucumber Raita* (page 180).

MAKES 8 SERVINGS.

Per Serving:
calories 185
protein 5 g
carbohydrates 30 g
fat 7 g

Nutrient Highlights:
calcium 109 mg
iron 4 mg

STIR-FRYING TIPS

1. Slice your vegetables before you begin cooking, since once you start stir-frying it proceeds very fast. For even cooking, keep all vegetable pieces about the same size and shape.

2. Heat your stir-fry pan or wok over fairly high heat. Your pan must be large enough to stir-fry all of your vegetables. I recommend using a wok, a traditional Chinese stir-fry pan. Woks are larger than frying pans and have sloping sides that make it a lot easier to stir the vegetables as they cook. You can also use specially shaped spatulas that have long handles and evenly toss the vegetables.

3. The best woks are heavy ones made of tempered steel. Some are sold pre-seasoned, with several sizes of stabilizing rings that fit underneath the wok.

HOW TO USE YOUR WOK

1. Pour in 1 Tbsp of unrefined oil. You require only a small amount of oil to keep your vegetables from sticking but its taste is very important. I prefer the flavours of toasted sesame or canola oil in stir fries.

2. Stir-fry onions, garlic, herbs and seeds first to give the stir fry a deep base-line flavour. When the oil sizzles, add onion, crushed garlic, minced fresh gingerroot. Stir-fry for 2 minutes. Then add dried herbs and seeds. One of my favourite mixtures for stir fries is thyme, rosemary and basil. Sesame seeds add flavour and colour. Stir constantly for 2 minutes more, using your wok spatula or a wooden spoon.

3. Add your vegetables, beginning with the hardest, densest textures first. Stir them rapidly around the wok, then put a cover on the wok to steam them for a few minutes. Next add the softer vegetables. As the cooking progresses, turn down the heat under the wok. If the vegetables start to stick, pour in a little water or soy sauce. As the vegetables continue to cook, add the softer vegetables, stirring quickly and covering the wok for a few minutes, then stirring more until all your vegetables are in the wok. DO NOT OVERCOOK!

4. Cook the stir fry until each vegetable is just done — crispy, brightly coloured and strong tasting. Never cook a vegetable until it is soft or mushy.

5. Wipe your wok out with a cloth. Never submerge in soapy water. Your wok will stay seasoned if you don't scrub it. Food will taste even more delicious and you will never have to use much oil.

STIR-FRY VEGETABLE CHART

Hard Vegetables: 12 to 15 minutes	*Medium Vegetables:* 8 to 10 minutes	*Soft Vegetables:* 3 to 4 minutes
broccoli	asparagus	Chinese cabbage
carrots	corn	fresh basil
cauliflower	eggplant	fresh parsley
celery	green peas	green onions
green or yellow beans	green peppers	spinach
kale	radishes	sprouts
potatoes	snow peas	Swiss chard
	zucchini	tomatoes

THE POWER WOK STIR FRY

The secret behind successful stir-frying in a wok is adding your ingredients in the right order. There has to be enough liquid to sauté or steam the ingredients. As vegetables soften, they release liquid. Always have 1/2 cup of water on hand. To speed things up, some people will steam certain vegetables ahead of time. Serve with brown rice, pasta or a baked potato.

PREPARATION TIME: 30 MINUTES

1 Tbsp toasted sesame oil *15 mL*
2 onions, sliced
2 cloves garlic, mashed
½ tsp dried rosemary, crushed *2 mL*
½ tsp dried basil *2 mL*
2 Tbsp mirin or rice wine vinegar *25 mL*
1 Tbsp sesame seeds *15 mL*
2 medium carrots, sliced diagonally
2 stalks broccoli, slices, florets
2 Tbsp soy sauce *25 mL*
6 oz mushrooms, sliced *200 g*
8 asparagus spears, cut in 2" (5 cm) pieces
½ bunch fresh spinach
1 red pepper, diced
8 oz tofu, cut in ½" (1.25 cm) cubes
¼ cup fresh basil leaves, slivered *50 mL*
½ cup fresh pineapple chunks *125 mL*

Heat oil in wok over high heat. Stir-fry onions, garlic, rosemary, basil, mirin and sesame seeds until onions start to brown.

Stir in carrots, broccoli, soy sauce and 2 Tbsp (25 mL)

water. Put lid on wok and cook 6 minutes, until just tender.

Add mushrooms and asparagus. Uncover, stir and cook about 5 minutes.

Add spinach, red pepper, tofu, basil and pineapple chunks. As soon as spinach is wilted, serve. Sprinkle with sesame seeds.

MAKES 6 SERVINGS.

Per Serving:
calories 155
protein 12 g
carbohydrates 20 g
fat 6 g

Nutrient Highlights:
calcium 252 mg
iron 7 mg
zinc 2 mg

Vegetable Shish Kebab

*At last! A recipe for the barbecue or broiler! Prepare the vegetables,
making sure that they are roughly the same size, approximately
1 ½" (3.75 cm), to ensure even cooking. Serve kebab over
rice, couscous or noodles, with chutney.*

PREPARATION TIME: 20 MINUTES
COOKING TIME: 12 MINUTES

8 9" (23 cm) bamboo skewers
1 pint cherry tomatoes *500 mL*
1 red pepper, cubed
1 green pepper, cubed
2 red onions, cubed
16 mushrooms
1 zucchini, halved lengthwise and cubed
3 potatoes or yams, cubed

MARINADE:

1 cup soy sauce *250 mL*
1 ½ cups water *375 mL*
3 Tbsp lightly toasted curry powder *45 mL*
2 Tbsp grated gingerroot *25 mL*
4 bay leaves, crushed
2 onions, thinly sliced
4 cloves garlic, thinly sliced

Soak skewers in cold water to cover for 1 hour.
Whisk together soy sauce, water, curry powder, ginger-
root, bay leaves, onion and garlic in large glass bowl.
Steam cubed potatoes or yams for 5 minutes.
Prepare vegetables, making sure that they are roughly the

same size. Marinate for 2 hours at room temperature.

Divide vegetables evenly on skewers, alternating to make a colourful arrangement. Grill kebabs over a greased, medium-high grill for about 12 minutes, turning and basting with left-over marinade, until tender-crisp.

Alternatively, broil for 8 minutes under broiler, also turning and basting.

MAKES 4 SERVINGS.

TIP: Cube 4 oz (125 g) tofu and add to kebabs for extra protein.

Per Serving:
calories 193
protein 9 g
carbohydrates 42 g
fat 2 g

Nutrient Highlights:
calcium 68 mg
iron 5 mg
zinc 1 mg

CUCUMBER RAITA

I love a delicious raita. So soothing to the taste buds.
Low-fat yogurt works just fine.

PREPARATION TIME: 10 MINUTES

½ large cucumber
2 Tbsp finely chopped onion *25 mL*
1 cup yogurt *250 mL*
pinch cayenne pepper
¼ *tsp* ground cumin *1 mL*
¼ *tsp* salt *1 mL*
chopped fresh coriander (or mint)

Peel cucumber, seed and coarsely grate. Stir together cucumber, onion and yogurt.

Stir in cayenne, cumin and salt. Add as much chopped coriander as you like.

Serve chilled. Especially good with curries (see our *Spinach-Zucchini Curry,* page 172).

MAKES 4 SERVINGS.

Per Serving:
calories 48
protein 3 g
carbohydrates 7 g
fat 1 g

Nutrient Highlights:
calcium 115 mg

PASTA DISHES

PASTA DISHES

PASTA IS ECONOMICAL AND NUTRITIOUS. It is a good source of carbohydrates and protein (six of the eight essential amino acids); it is also low in fat and calories. There are now a wide range of pastas available, both fresh and dried. Some companies are marketing a variety of pastas made from several types of grain.

I don't want to sound like a snob, but Italian dried pasta is of a better quality than those made domestically. They have been making pasta for a very long time for a very fussy, tradition-conscious public. Italian pasta is firmer and uses top-quality ingredients.

Pasta is formed from a paste of high gluten flour — durum wheat semolina flour — moistened with water, sometimes with egg. The dough is squeezed between rollers until it is a densely compacted sheet. The harder the dough is rolled, the better "bite" the pasta will have when it is cooked. Shaped pastas such as shells, rotini and wheels are very easy to cook.

Most of the wheat flour in Japanese pasta is milled from soft (as opposed to hard) wheat. Japanese pasta has a lower gluten content and a much softer texture than European-style pasta. Japanese pasta also cooks very quickly — within five minutes. Other "healthy" pastas will often have a gritty texture due to the bran content of the flour and, as a result, don't please everyone. You taste and you choose.

A lot of fresh pastas are more expensive than their dried counterparts. My rule is: good, fresh pasta should be made locally and recently. Check the date!

Pasta combines well with beans and vegetables. We add pesto and curry paste to our pasta to add flavour but not fat. A minimum amount of oil or butter will go a long way.

ALL PURPOSE PASTA

PREPARATION TIME: 15 MINUTES

1 tsp dried basil *5 mL*
½ tsp dried rosemary *2 mL*
2 Tbsp olive oil *25 mL*
1 lb pasta *500 g*
2 Tbsp unsalted butter *25 mL*
1 Tbsp lemon juice *15 mL*

Fill soup pot (or any large pot) about two-thirds full of water. Add basil and rosemary; bring to a boil.

Add oil and pasta. Return to a boil, stir once and cover. Turn heat to low.

Stir twice to keep from sticking to bottom of pot. Cook until pasta is al dente — usually 8 to 12 minutes for dried pasta, 3 to 4 minutes for fresh or frozen pasta. The best way to tell if pasta is done is to take out a piece and bite it. It's done when it is cooked through except for a tiny hard core right at the centre.

Pour pasta into colander to drain, but do not rinse. The butter and lemon juice will stick better to the pasta if you haven't rinsed all the starch away. Return pasta to cooking pot and toss in butter and lemon juice.

MAKES 4 SERVINGS.

Per Serving:
calories 504
protein 14 g
carbohydrates 80 g
fat 14 g

Nutrient Highlights:
iron 4 g
zinc 1.5 g

Herb Pesto

What to do with leftover fresh herbs and salad greens? Turn them into a pesto! Since all too often I have leftover herbs, it makes me feel very thrifty to make pesto. I add pesto to soups and spread it on toast and bagels. So many uses! If you want to make this recipe dairy-free, use good-tasting nutritional yeast instead of Parmesan cheese.

PREPARATION TIME: 20 MINUTES

½ cup pine nuts *125 mL*
3 cloves garlic
¾ cup freshly grated Parmesan cheese *175 mL*
¼ tsp salt *1 mL*
3 cups combination lightly packed fresh basil,
spinach, dill, parsley and chives *750 mL*
2 Tbsp olive oil *25 mL*

Measure all ingredients into blender or food processor.
Blend until smooth, scraping down sides.
Taste and adjust seasoning.

MAKES 2 CUPS (500 mL).

Keeps up to 3 weeks in the refrigerator; do not add cheese and cover with a thin layer of olive oil. Keeps up to 6 weeks in the freezer.

Per ¼ Cup Serving:
calories 118
protein 6 g
carbohydrates 3 g
fat 10 g

Nutrient Highlights:
calcium 130 mg
iron 2 mg
zinc 1 mg

Pasta & Pesto

PREPARATION TIME: 20 MINUTES

1 lb pasta *500 g*
1 ½ cup pesto *250 mL*
1 cup vegetable stock *250 mL*
2 Tbsp lemon juice *25 mL*
¼ tsp ground black pepper *1 mL*
2 Tbsp freshly grated cheese *25 mL*
2 tomatoes, chopped

Cook, drain and season pasta according to *All Purpose Pasta* instructions on page 184.

Return cooked pasta to pot over medium heat. Add 1 cup of the pesto; stir constantly while pesto coats pasta. Gradually stir in stock.

Add lemon juice and pepper.

Serve a mound of hot pasta on each plate. Sprinkle with cheese, then with tomatoes. Put a tablespoon of the remaining pesto right in the middle.

MAKES 4 SERVINGS.

TIP: For a creamy pasta, substitute 1 cup (250 mL) milk or soy milk for vegetable stock.

Per Serving:
calories 614
protein 24 g
carbohydrates 90 g
fat 19 g

Nutrient Highlights:
calcium 258 mg
iron 7 mg
zinc 3 mg

Sun-Dried Tomato Purée

This purée can replace everyday tomato paste. When mixed with plain grains, it provides a tasty layer in any casserole. Dried tomatoes that haven't been packed in oil often have a dense, leathery texture. They are also a lot less expensive than the oil-packed imports. I like to make a thick purée out of them and use it in place of tomato paste. There are no added seasonings, just the concentrated flavour of the tomatoes. Only use the olive oil if you want to refrigerate for later use. What a relief from regular tomato paste! (See Shells with Spinach and Chick-peas.)

PREPARATION TIME: 20 MINUTES

¾ cup sun-dried tomatoes *175 mL*
1 cup water *250 mL*
2 tsp extra virgin olive oil *10 mL*

Bring tomatoes and water to a boil in small, heavy-bottomed saucepan. Reduce heat and simmer gently for 15 minutes.

Transfer tomatoes and their liquid to food processor or blender. Process for several minutes until sauce is smooth, adding more water if necessary.

Pack purée into clean jar. Cover the top with olive oil. Cover jar tightly.

MAKES ¾ CUP (175 mL).

Keeps up to 1 week in the refrigerator.

Per ¼ Cup Serving:
calories 52
protein 1 g
carbohydrates 6 g
fat 3 g

SOBA NORI ROLLS

*Noodles wrapped in nori! Why not? Chewy, moist little bites that can
be an appetizer or main course. It's become a family favourite.
Jim, my partner in life, creates a dipping sauce that he thinks is
essential, so here it is: mix a few tablespoons of soy sauce with
1 teaspoon of dry wasabi powder and 1 tablespoon of water. Mix
it all together, and dip away. In a pinch I have substituted spaghetti
for the soba noodles and my Sun-Dried Tomato Purée
(see page 187) and crumbled cheese for the plum paste.*

PREPARATION TIME: 20 MINUTES

½ English cucumber
8 oz soba noodles *250 g*
4 sheets nori
1 Tbsp wasabi powder *15 mL*
1 tsp umebushi plum paste *5 mL*
1 Tbsp water *15 mL*
pickled ginger

Quarter cucumber lengthwise and cut into ¼" (.6 cm)
strips the length of the nori sheets.

Cook soba noodles in boiling water about 5 minutes or
until al dente. Drain, rinse thoroughly, and drain again very
well. Place noodles on paper towel and block to absorb excess
moisture. Place 1 sheet of nori on sushi mat. Arrange mat so
that long end is facing you. Divide soba noodles into 4
batches. Line up noodles to cover nori sheet.

Mix wasabi powder and umebushi plum paste with water
to make paste. Using index finger, smear 1 tsp (5 mL) paste
in strip across nori, 1" (2.5 cm) from bottom edge of nori.

Place 2 cucumber strips on top of paste strip.

To roll, lift sushi mat and begin to roll up, holding filling in place with index fingers. Roll nori neatly and firmly, like a jelly roll, almost to the end. Moisten top strip of nori with water to seal the roll.

Trim off excess noodles and cucumber sticking out ends of roll with sharp knife. Slice roll into 5 pieces.

MAKES 20 PIECES.

Per Roll:
calories 21
protein 1 g
carbohydrates 4 g
fat - g

Shells with Spinach & Chick-peas

A one bowl meal! People are always asking for simple, very-few-pots-in-a-meal recipes. All you need for this one is a wok (or large skillet) and a cooking pot: this is as simple as I can get. The shells are delicious hot or cold. Stuff this mixture in a pita bread and you have a hearty meal. Other greens can be used — Swiss chard, kale, water cress — just finely chop them. See page 187 for the Sun-Dried Tomato Purée recipe.

PREPARATION TIME: 25 MINUTES

2 Tbsp extra virgin olive oil *25 mL*
2 cloves garlic, minced
1 onion, finely chopped
2 carrots, finely shredded
1 cup finely chopped parsley or basil *250 mL*
½ tsp salt *2 mL*
¾ cup Sun-Dried Tomato Purée *175 mL*
1 ½ cups cooked chick-peas *375 mL*
1 ½ cups spinach leaves, washed and chopped *375 mL*
¼ cup bean liquid *50 mL*
½ lb medium-sized pasta shells *250 g*
¼ tsp freshly ground pepper *1 mL*
½ cup freshly grated cheese *125 mL*

Heat olive oil in wok. Add garlic, onion, carrots and parsley. Cook for 5 minutes. Season with salt. Add tomato purée, chick-peas, spinach and 1 cup (250 mL) of water or cooking liquid from the chick-peas. Lower heat and simmer until vegetables are tender-crisp while the pasta is cooking.

Bring a large pot of water to boil. Add pasta; stir and cook until al dente. Drain pasta and return to pot. Toss with cooked vegetables and chick-peas and season with pepper and cheese. Serve with more freshly grated cheese or good-tasting nutritional yeast.

MAKES 4 SERVINGS.

Per Serving:
calories 457
protein 19 g
carbohydrates 70 g
fat 13 g

Nutrient Highlights:
calcium 230 mg
iron 5 mg
zinc 2 mg

THAI CURRY NOODLE

All too often ingredients imported from Thailand (especially in cans) are very old, oily and use preservatives. My favourite brand of Thai curry paste is Thai Kitchen — no preservatives, delicious and fresh. You can use any type of thin noodle in this dish; kids love it. For the fat content conscious, note that low-fat coconut milk is also available.

PREPARATION TIME: 20 MINUTES

2 Tbsp canola oil *25 mL*
2 onions, thinly sliced
1 Tbsp Thai curry paste *15 mL*
½ cup vegetable stock or water *125 mL*
2 large red peppers, coarsely chopped
1 bunch broccoli, cut into small florets
2 cups coconut milk *500 mL*
1 ½ lb vermicelli *750 g*
2 Tbsp fresh coriander, finely chopped *25 mL*

Heat oil in large skillet over medium-high heat. Cook onions for 5 minutes, or until translucent.

Add curry paste and stir until evenly distributed. Add stock and bring to a boil. Add peppers and broccoli. Lower heat and simmer, covered, for 5 minutes, or until tender-crisp. Remove from heat and keep warm.

Meanwhile, cook vermicelli according to package directions. While vermicelli is draining, add coconut milk to vegetables in skillet and return to very low heat. As soon as coconut milk is mixed in with sauce, add vermicelli and stir gently to coat with sauce. Garnish with coriander.

MAKES 6 TO 8 SERVINGS.

Per Serving:
calories 444
protein 15 g
carbohydrates 70 g
fat 17 g

Nutrient Highlights:
calcium 77 mg
iron 6 mg
zinc 2 mg

DESSERTS

DESSERTS

ORIGINALLY I DIDN'T want to include a section featuring desserts, but everyone I know enjoys dessert. My ideal dessert is a ripe piece of fresh fruit, a slice of chilled melon. However, my mother grew up in a bake shop, and all my life I have eaten the freshest, tastiest cakes and cookies. Thinking of my Zimmerman grandparents toiling away baking, I just can't leave out this section.

Dessert does not have to be fussy or rely on expensive ingredients. Although people have a laissez-faire attitude towards just how fattening a dessert can be ("It's *dessert!*" they say), we want to keep the calories at a modest level. I have tried to minimize the amount of dairy and oil. You can replace the eggs in any of these recipes with flax seeds. See page 203 for detailed instructions.

Many of the recipes included I developed with my kids: gingersnaps, peanut butter cookies, popcorn balls and sesame banana cookies. So if they ask, "Is there cake in the house?", the answer is yes, and may it be a delicious, healthy one.

· ✳ ·

DATE BREAD

This cake is so moist and chewy that I don't want to eat anything else all day. Take it along when you're hiking or having other adventures in the outdoors, and when you need some energy, have a slice. I've used apple cider and apple strawberry juice instead of plain apple juice and things tasted just fine.

PREPARATION TIME: 20 MINUTES

COOKING TIME: 1 HOUR

½ cup boiling apple juice *125 mL*

1 cup chopped dates *250 mL*

2 cups whole wheat pastry flour *500 mL*

1 tsp baking powder *5 mL*

1 tsp baking soda *5 mL*

½ tsp salt *2 mL*

½ cup honey *125 mL*

⅓ cup canola oil *75 mL*

2 Tbsp grated orange rind *25 mL*

2 Tbsp orange juice *25 mL*

1 small banana, chopped

½ cup chopped pecans *125 mL*

Preheat oven to 350°F (180°C).

Pour apple juice over dates and let soak for 10 minutes. Purée until smooth in food processor or blender.

Sift together flour, baking powder, baking soda and salt in large bowl.

In medium bowl, mix together honey, oil, orange rind and orange juice until well combined. Stir in banana and pecans.

Make a well in centre of flour mixture and pour in liquids, stirring until just blended.

Pour into 9" x 5" (1.5 L) greased loaf pan. Bake for 1 hour, or until cake tester comes out clean.

MAKES 1 LOAF.

Per Serving:
calories 254
protein 4 g
carbohydrates 42 g
fat 10 g

Nutrient Highlights:
zinc 1 mg

APPLE CRISP

I was in a restaurant that shall remain nameless. There they served the worst piece of apple crisp imaginable. After patiently listening to my carping, my husband Jim told me to come up with my own version. (He insisted on eating his piece with ice cream.)

PREPARATION TIME: 20 MINUTES
COOKING TIME: 40 MINUTES

2 lbs organic Spy or Macintosh apples 1 Kg
¾ tsp cinnamon 3 mL
¼ tsp ground coriander 1 mL
pinch salt
1 ½ cups apple cider or juice 375 mL
2 cups rolled oats 500 mL
½ cup whole wheat pastry flour 125 mL
½ cup chopped pecans or walnuts 125 mL
¼ cup canola oil 50 mL
2 Tbsp maple syrup 25 mL
pinch salt

Preheat oven to 350°F (180°C).

Rinse apples; quarter and core. Slice crosswise thinly. Place apples in 9" x 9" (23 cm x 23 cm) baking dish. Toss with cinnamon, coriander, salt and cider.

Mix together oats, flour, pecans, oil, maple syrup and salt. Press down gently over apples.

Bake for 40 minutes, or until crust is crunchy and apples are soft.

MAKES 6 SERVINGS.

Per Serving:
calories 420
protein 7 g
carbohydrates 62 g
fat 18 g

Nutrient Highlights:
calcium 47 mg
iron 2 mg
zinc 2 mg

LEMON POPPY SEED CAKE

The secret for this recipe is to add lemon rind to the poppy seed/milk mixture and the wet ingredients. A distinct but subtle lemon taste comes through, and it makes the cake a delicious slice of enjoyment. I often use vanilla soy milk instead of regular milk.

PREPARATION TIME: 20 MINUTES

COOKING TIME: 40 MINUTES

1 cup poppy seeds *250 mL*
2 cups milk *500 mL*
1 Tbsp grated lemon rind *15 mL*
½ cup butter *125 mL*
½ cup honey *125 mL*
½ cup granulated sugar *125 mL*
2 eggs
1 tsp vanilla *5 mL*
1 cup whole wheat pastry flour *250 mL*
1 cup unbleached white flour *250 mL*
1 Tbsp baking powder *15 mL*
½ tsp salt *2 mL*

Preheat oven to 375°F (190°C).

Combine poppy seeds and 1⅓ cup (325 mL) of the milk with 1 tsp (5 mL) of the lemon zest in saucepan. Bring to a boil, then remove from heat and allow to steep for 20 minutes.

Meanwhile, cream together butter, honey and sugar with electric mixer. Beat in eggs, vanilla, remaining milk and remaining lemon zest.

Mix together flours, baking powder and salt in large bowl.

Combine cooled poppy seed mixture with other liquids and stir into dry ingredients just until moist.

Pour into greased 10" (25 cm) springform pan. Bake 40 minutes, or until cake tester comes out clean. Allow to cool in pan, then run knife around edge and remove springform sides.

MAKES 10 SERVINGS.

TIP: Flax seeds can be used to replace eggs in baking. Grind your flax seeds in a spice or coffee grinder. For each egg, measure 1 Tbsp (15 mL) ground flax seed, and add 3 Tbsp (45 mL) water. Stir and allow to thicken for 5 minutes. Add to other wet ingredients. For larger quantities, purée 1 cup of flax seeds and store in freezer.

Per Serving:
calories 320
protein 7 g
carbohydrates 46 g
fat 13 g

Nutrient Highlights:
calcium 160 mg
iron 2 mg
zinc 1 mg

CARROT CAKE

No vegetarian cookbook would be complete without a carrot cake and icing recipe. Carrots are an affordable organic staple. This cake will stay fresh for several days. Its light, moist texture is delicious paired with icing or all on its own.

PREPARATION TIME: 15 MINUTES
COOKING TIME: 30 MINUTES

2 *cups* whole wheat pastry flour *500 mL*
1 *Tbsp* baking powder *15 mL*
1 *tsp* ground cardamom *5 mL*
1 *tsp* cinnamon *5 mL*
½ *tsp* sea salt *2 mL*
1 *cup* honey *250 mL*
½ *cup* canola oil *125 mL*
3 eggs
¼ *cup* milk *50 mL*
1 *tsp* vanilla *5 mL*
2 carrots, grated

Preheat oven to 375°F (190°C).

Stir together flour, baking powder, cardamom, cinnamon and salt in large bowl.

In medium bowl, beat honey together with oil. Beat in eggs one at a time. Add milk and vanilla; stir in carrots.

Pour over dry ingredients and stir until thoroughly combined.

Pour into greased 9" x 13" (3.5 L) pan. Bake for 30 minutes or until golden brown and cake tester comes out clean.

MAKES 12 SERVINGS.

Per Serving:
calories 354
protein 7 g
carbohydrates 44 g
fat 19 g

Nutrient Highlights:
calcium 54 mg
iron 2 mg
zinc 1 mg

CREAM CHEESE ICING

PREPARATION TIME: 10 MINUTES

6 oz cream cheese *200 g*
2 Tbsp honey *25 mL*
¾ tsp vanilla *3 mL*
2 Tbsp orange juice *25 mL*
½ cup chopped nuts *125 mL*

Beat together cream cheese, honey, vanilla and orange juice until light and creamy using electric mixer.
Spread on cake with spatula. Sprinkle with chopped nuts.

MAKES 1 CUP (250 mL) — ENOUGH TO ICE 9" x 13" (3.5 L) CAKE.

Per Serving:
calories 107
protein 4 g
carbohydrates 7 g
fat 8 g

COCONUT CAKE

I like a moist cake when I eat cake. The coconut and raisins in this recipe give a chewy filling that satisfies my cake soul. Thank you, Helen Cronish, for your inspiration and fellow appreciation of coconut.

PREPARATION TIME: 15 MINUTES
COOKING TIME 30 MINUTES

1 ½ cups whole wheat pastry flour *375 mL*
½ cup wheat germ *125 mL*
1 Tbsp grated orange zest *15 mL*
1 Tbsp baking powder *15 mL*
2 tsp cinnamon *10 mL*
½ tsp nutmeg *2 mL*
½ tsp salt *2 mL*
1 cup unsweetened shredded coconut *250 mL*
¾ cup raisins *175 mL*
3 eggs
¾ cup honey *175 mL*
½ cup canola oil *125 mL*
1 cup milk *250 mL*

Preheat oven to 375°F (190°C).

Combine flour, wheat germ, orange zest, baking powder, cinnamon, nutmeg and salt in large bowl. Stir in coconut and raisins.

In medium bowl, beat eggs until foamy. Whisk in honey, oil and milk. Pour over dry ingredients; stir until just combined.

Bake in a greased 10" (25 cm) tube pan for about 30 minutes or until golden brown and cake tester comes out clean.

MAKES 10 SERVINGS.

Tip: Serve with a warm fruit compote.

Per Serving:
calories 376
protein 7 g
carbohydrates 50 g
fat 19 g

Nutrient Highlights:
calcium 74 mg
iron 2 mg
zinc 2 mg

Peanut Butter Cookies

My daughter Mackenzie loves peanut butter cookies — she would eat the entire batter if she could. She bakes at her school, The School House, and feels very relaxed in any kitchen.

PREPARATION TIME: 15 MINUTES

½ cup butter, softened *125 mL*
⅔ cup honey *150 mL*
1 ¼ cups peanut butter *300 mL*
3 Tbsp milk *45 mL*
1 tsp vanilla *5 mL*
2 ¾ cups whole wheat pastry flour *675 mL*
1 tsp baking soda *5 mL*
½ tsp salt *2 mL*

Preheat oven to 325°F (160°C).

Cream butter and honey with electric mixer. Add peanut butter, milk and vanilla. Beat until smooth.

In separate bowl, stir flour, baking soda and salt together. Stir into peanut butter mixture by hand.

Using 1 Tbsp (15 mL) batter per cookie, roll into balls and place on lightly greased or parchment-paper lined baking sheets 2" (5 cm) apart. Set tines of fork across cookie and gently push down. Then cross the cookie with the fork again. Bake 12 to 15 minutes, rotating sheets in oven half-way through baking. Bake until lightly brown.

MAKES APPROXIMATELY 4 DOZEN.

Per Serving:
calories 95
protein 3 g
carbohydrates 10 g
fat 5 g

GINGERSNAPS

My kids go to a terrific alternative private school called The School House that provides a supportive, fun and egalitarian environment in which to learn. Among their activities, the kids have the opportunity to bake and learn basic cooking skills. I have included this recipe, with a little adaptation, from their repertoire of delicious desserts.

PREPARATION TIME: 15 MINUTES
COOKING TIME: 10 MINUTES

⅓ *cup* canola oil *75 mL*
½ *cup* fancy molasses *125 mL*
½ *cup* honey *125 mL*
½ *cup* packed brown sugar *125 mL*
1 egg white
1 egg
1 cup whole wheat pastry flour *250 mL*
2 cups unbleached flour *500 mL*
1 ½ tsp baking soda *7 mL*
½ *tsp* salt *2 mL*
2 tsp ground ginger *10 mL*
½ *tsp* cinnamon *2 mL*
½ *tsp* ground cardamom *2 mL*

Preheat oven to 375°F (190°C).

Beat oil, molasses, honey, sugar, egg and egg white with electric mixer until smooth and frothy.

In separate bowl, sift together flours, baking soda, salt, ginger, cinnamon and cardamom.

Stir dry ingredients into wet until thoroughly combined.

Bake on lightly greased, or parchment-paper lined baking sheets for 10 minutes or until lightly browned.

MAKES ABOUT 5 DOZEN COOKIES.

Keeps 3 days in an airtight container.

Per Cookie:
calories 56
protein 1 g
carbohydrates 10 g
fat 1 g

Sesame Banana Cookies

Lining your baking sheets with parchment paper instead of greasing them helps cut down on fat. I like to toast sesame seeds against parchment paper. It can be used and reused to line baking sheets. Toasting seeds creates a subtle aroma in the air....

PREPARATION TIME: 15 MINUTES
COOKING TIME: 10 MINUTES

1 cup sesame seeds *250 mL*
2 cups whole wheat pastry flour *500 mL*
1 tsp baking powder *5 mL*
1 tsp salt *5 mL*
½ tsp ground nutmeg *2 mL*
½ cup unsalted butter *125 mL*
½ cup honey *125 mL*
2 ripe bananas, mashed
1 egg
1 tsp vanilla *5 mL*

Preheat oven to 350° (180°C).

Spread sesame seeds on baking sheet and toast 5 minutes or until lightly browned. Cool.

Sift together flour, baking powder, salt and nutmeg in medium bowl.

In large bowl, cream butter and honey with electric mixer until fluffy. Beat in bananas, egg, and vanilla.

Add dry ingredients to banana mixture one-third at a time, mixing well after each addition. Stir in toasted sesame seeds.

Drop by the teaspoonful onto lightly greased baking sheets. Bake for 8 to 10 minutes or until lightly golden.

MAKES APPROXIMATELY 3 DOZEN.

TIP: Smooth cookies before baking using a wet palette knife.

Per Cookie
calories 90
protein 2 g
carbohydrates 11 g
fat 5 g

Tofu Apple Kugel

A kugel is an Eastern European pudding that is usually made with potatoes, noodles or cheese. A traditional kugel never contains tofu, so when I serve a piece to my favourite Aunt Jenny, she always marvels at how delicious it is. Kugel can be served hot or cold, and is a delight for kids. A great way to use up left-over tofu.

PREPARATION TIME: 15 MINUTES
COOKING TIME: 45 MINUTES

1 lb tofu *500 g*
½ cup vanilla yogurt *125 mL*
⅓ cup maple syrup *75 mL*
2 Tbsp almond butter *25 mL*
2 Tbsp lemon juice *25 mL*
1 tsp ground cinnamon *5 mL*
1 tsp vanilla *5 mL*
½ tsp ground coriander *2 mL*
2 apples, peeled and thinly sliced
2 cups raspberries *500 mL*
¼ cup sliced almonds, toasted *50 mL*
¼ cup shredded coconut *50 mL*

Preheat oven to 325° F(160°C).

Blend tofu in food processor or blender until smooth. Add yogurt, maple syrup, almond butter, lemon juice, cinnamon, vanilla and coriander. Blend until smooth.

Transfer tofu mixture to bowl and stir in apples, raspberries and almonds.

Turn into lightly greased 11" x 7" (28 cm x 17 cm) baking dish and sprinkle with coconut.

Bake covered for 45 minutes or until set. Let stand 10 minutes before serving.

Makes 6 servings.

Tip: Use any combination of seasonal fruit equalling 4 cups (1L). If fresh fruit is scarce, use 3 apples and ½ cup (125 mL) raisins, dried blueberries or cranberries.

Per Serving:
calories 212
protein 4 g
carbohydrates 32 g
fat 9 g

Nutrient Highlights:
calcium 108 mg
iron 2 mg
zinc 1 mg

Tofu Cocoa Pie

*Chocolate lovers consider tofu and cocoa a stretch of the imagination.
But if you're looking for ways to combine ingredients in new and
inventive ways, this no-bake, dairy-free tofu (dare I call it cheesecake?)
is a light, tasty introduction to a world of desserts.
Carob can be substituted for cocoa.*

PREPARATION TIME: 20 MINUTES
CHILLING TIME: 1 HOUR

CRUST:

1 ⅓ cups finely ground graham cracker crumbs *325 mL*
¼ cup canola oil *50 mL*
1 tsp cinnamon *5 mL*

Blend graham crackers with oil and cinnamon. Mix well.
Press mixture into bottom and sides of a 9" (23 cm) glass
pie plate. Chill thoroughly for 20 minutes in refrigerator
before filling.

FILLING:

¾ cup maple syrup *175 mL*
⅓ cup cocoa *75 mL*
2 tsp vanilla *10 mL*
1/2 tsp cinnamon *2 mL*
1½ lb tofu, pressed *750 g*
2 Tbsp agar-agar flakes *25 mL*

Combine maple syrup, cocoa, vanilla, cinnamon and
tofu in food processor until very smooth. (See page 129 for
detailed instructions on pressing tofu.)
Bring ½ cup (125 mL) water to a boil. Add agar-agar

flakes and stir until dissolved. Simmer for 3 minutes, stirring occasionally, until thickened. Add to filling mixture and blend in food processor until very smooth.

Pour into chilled pie shell and refrigerate for 1 hour, loosely covered, until firm.

TIP: Use your favourite cookie wafer to make the crust: gingersnaps or vanilla wafers work well (1 ⅓ cups/325 mL = approximately 4 oz/125 g wafers).

Per Serving:
calories 296
protein 9 g
carbohydrates 39 g
fat 14 g

Nutrient Highlights:
calcium 142 mg
iron 6 mg
zinc 1 mg

Basmati Rice & Coconut Milk Pudding

This is equally good warm or chilled for breakfast. Hollow out a cantaloupe and fill it with rice and fresh fruit — some of my friends have been known to splash it with various liqueurs. Use a variety of diced fruit, according to availability: mango, kiwi, papaya, pineapple, pears, melon. It's a satisfying fruit salad freshly prepared or chilled. Low-fat coconut milk is widely available; vanilla soy milk is a good substitute for coconut milk as well.

PREPARATION TIME: 30 MINUTES
COOKING TIME: 35 MINUTES

1 cup basmati rice *250 mL*
1 cinnamon stick
pinch salt
2 cups coconut milk *500 mL*
4 cups diced fruit *1 L*
2 Tbsp coarsely chopped pistachios *25 mL*
ground cinnamon

Rinse rice well. Cover with cold water and soak for 10 minutes; drain.

Bring rice, cinnamon stick and 2 cups (500 mL) water to a boil. Reduce heat and simmer gently for about 15 minutes, or until water has been absorbed.

Stir in salt and coconut milk; bring to a boil. Reduce heat and simmer gently, stirring occasionally, for 20 minutes or until rice is tender.

Discard cinnamon stick. When cooled slightly, fold in fruit and sprinkle with nuts and ground cinnamon to taste.

MAKES 8 SERVINGS.

Per Serving:
calories 228
protein 4 g
carbohydrates 35 g
fat 14 g

Nutrient Highlights:
iron 4 mg

ANTS ON A LOG

Kids love to cook. My son Cameron enjoys most organizing the bundles of ingredients. Fill a celery cavity with your favourite spread, top it off with seeds, nuts or raisins.

PREPARATION TIME: 5 MINUTES

3 celery stalks
½ cup cream cheese (at room temperature) *125 mL*
¼ cup raisins *50 mL*

Cut each celery in two.
Fill the cavity of each piece with cream cheese.
Top with raisins.

MAKES 6 LOGS.

Per Serving:
calories 93
protein 2 g
carbohydrates 7 g
fat 7 g

Honey Maple Popcorn Balls

A great way to use up leftover popcorn.

PREPARATION TIME: 25 MINUTES

⅓ cup liquid honey 75 mL
¼ cup water 50 mL
¼ cup maple syrup 50 mL
7 to 8 cups air-popped popcorn 2 to 2.5 L

Place honey, water and maple syrup in medium-sized saucepan over medium-high heat. Boil uncovered without stirring, until thick, about 8 to 9 minutes.

Meanwhile, place popcorn in large bowl. Pour syrup over popcorn. Toss using 1 or 2 large spoons until popcorn is evenly coated. With lightly buttered or oiled hands, form popcorn into ten 3" (7.5 cm) balls.

Gobble up right away or wrap in wax paper and store at room temperature.

MAKES 10 LARGE POPCORN BALLS.

Per Serving:
calories 78
protein 1 g
carbohydrates 19 g
fat - g

GLOSSARY OF INGREDIENTS

ADZUKI BEANS: small, striped maroon beans which are quick-cooking, and are a good source of B vitamins, potassium, iron and calcium; cook with kombu.

AGAR-AGAR: a taste-free vegetarian jelling agent made from sea vegetables, sold in the form of flakes or bars; makes a firm gel which sets at room temperature or, for a shorter setting time, in the refrigerator.

ARAME: a mild flavoured, thin-sliced sea vegetable resembling black spaghetti when sold in pre-cooked dried form; to use, soak in room temperature water for 5 minutes (save soaking water to use as plant food); used in soups, salads and casseroles.

BASMATI RICE: a type of long grain rice that has a delicate aroma and nut-like taste that suits many cuisines; parboiled cooks in 20 minutes. Brown organic basmati rice offers a nice alternative to long grain brown rice; requires 45 minutes to cook.

BUCKWHEAT: an edible fruit seed related to rhubarb; the three-cornered seed has a black outer hull that is removed to reveal a tan-coloured kernel that is used for cereal, flour and stock feed; high in protein, B vitamins, calcium and iron. Low in gluten, buckwheat must be mixed with wheat flour to make bread. When boiled, buckwheat groats swell and lose their shape. Some chefs (my mother) combine an egg with the uncooked groats and the groats retain their shape — blame it on the egg albumin.

BULGUR: made from wheat berries that have been precooked, dried and cracked; when cracked small brown grit-like pieces are created. Medium ground bulgur is preferred for its nice chewy texture. Add boiling water to bulgur, cover and 15 minutes later the grain has absorbed the water and is ready to use. Never rinse bulgur; it will turn to mush.

CELERIAC: a tough, knobby root (also known as celery root) often sold caked with dirt; resembles parsley and celery in flavour; can be cooked like turnip; used in soups and stews or grated raw on salads.

COUSCOUS: North-African staple made from semolina (the starch of durum wheat); the semolina is ground, mixed with water into strands, cut into small pieces, steamed and dried; cooks quickly. Read your labels to check whether your brand of couscous has the bran and germ intact; it makes it into a nutritious food item.

DAIKON: a very long, hairy, white radish with a hot taste that combines well with beans and greens; when cooked, its taste changes from hot to sweet; often shredded to eat with sushi or salad and pickled with other vegetables.

FLAX SEEDS: grinding these glossy brown seeds improves their digestibility. An excellent source of Vitamin E and Omega-3 fatty acids, they also make a good replacement for eggs in baking. (See page 129.) Store in freezer for up to three months.

HIJIKI: a strong-flavoured, dark-coloured sea vegetable that looks like thin angel hair pasta; high in calcium; grows close to the ocean bottom; can be very dirty, so rinse carefully.

KASHA: buckwheat groats; see *Buckwheat*.

KOMBU: a seaweed containing glutamic acid that is used as a soup and stock base; sold dried in flat sheets or in strips that measure between 6 to 8 inches (15 to 20 cm); may have a white powdery coating which contains lots of flavour, so do not rinse before cooking.

KUGEL: a wonderful word for a pudding that can contain any number of ingredients, usually vegetables and pasta (mine uses fruit and tofu).

LATKE: a potato (or sweet potato) pancake.

LEMON ZEST: the aromatic, yellow skin of lemons, not the bitter white inner pith.

LEMONGRASS: a delicate, lemony flavoured scent distinguishes this herb from all others. To buy the freshest lemongrass, press your nail into the centre to ensure that it feels damp. A trimmed stalk provides 2 tablespoons of finely chopped herb. Trim by cutting off the top of the stalk and the root end and removing the outside leaves.

MIRIN: a clear, sweet Japanese rice cooking wine that can be used in soups, stews, stir fries and dips.

MISO: salty Japanese paste made by cooking soybeans and mixing them with grains such as barley. Buy unpasteurized miso, which must be stored in the refrigerator; it has better flavour and nutritional value. Avoid boiling miso — it will destroy its enzymes.

NORI: a seaweed that is dried into thin, brittle, green sheets used for rolling sushi and as a garnish; must be kept dry or will tear easily. Buy nori that is labelled toasted.

NUTRITIONAL YEAST: not to be confused with baking yeast, this is not a leavening agent but a condiment that is added to casseroles for its nutritional value and cheese-like flavour.

PINE NUTS: small seeds from pine cones; store in refrigerator or freezer since they go rancid quickly.

QUINOA: (pronounced keen-wa) a small, high protein seed native to South America, the shape, colour and size of millet; in addition to protein, also provides starch, sugars, oil, fibre, minerals and vitamins.

SEITAN: wheat gluten that has been extracted from whole wheat flour with water; also known as "wheat meat." Check for expiry date on package. If you drain the seitan, reserve the liquid and add to pan.

SESAME OIL, TOASTED: made from toasted sesame seeds, this oil is darker in colour than plain sesame oil, with a wonderful aroma.

SESAME SEEDS: see *Tahini.*

SHIITAKE MUSHROOMS: available fresh or dried; Japanese mushrooms with a chewy texture and a distinct flavour. To rehydrate dried shiitake, boil for 5 minutes; remove and discard the tough stems and use the soaking liquid in soup broth.

SOY MILK: (vanilla or original) a non-dairy beverage derived from cooked, strained soybeans; used for drinking or cooking; flavourings sometimes added.

SURIBACHI: serrated ceramic bowl used with a wooden pestle or rod to crush seeds or mix misos or nut butters with broths.

TAHINI: ground sesame seed paste. Store sesame seeds in a sealed container in the refrigerator; they are very perishable due to their oil content.

TEMPEH: a high protein soy food made by fermenting crushed cooked soybeans which have been inoculated with the bacteria *rhizospirus oligosporus;* delicious marinated, grilled, stir-fried or oven roasted; must be cooked before eating.

TOFU: also know as bean curd; a mixture of soybeans, water and coagulant; easy to digest; store in refrigerator.

INDEX